THE STRUGGLE FOR SURVIVAL

This terse and dramatic account of England's most catastrophic years shows how she has adjusted to the conditions of a new world. In the first half of the twentieth century, England passed from a position of unrivaled economic strength and unchallenged national power through two wars that threatened her existence and led to the emergence of Russia and the United States as greater powers.

During this crucial time, England defended her democracy against dictation from abroad—and from the menace of world domination by Hitler. After World War II her empire gradually dissolved into the far-spread British Commonwealth—a new political structure that threads British democracy across the world.

The author's account moves from the days of Gladstone, Disraeli, and Lord Salisbury to those of Asquith, Lloyd George, and Churchill. He records England's history from the First World War to her new position in a world that faces the universal threat of nuclear and biologic weapons, the challenge of survival in the twentieth century.

The text includes a bibliography for recommended reading, a chronological table of events, and illustrations.

Other MENTOR Books on English History

A Short History of 16th Century England: 1485-1603 by *G. W. O. Woodward*

How the Tudor monarchs from Henry VII to Elizabeth I suppressed the medieval church; brought order to a politically chaotic land, and launched overseas exploration that was to result in the far-reaching power of the British Empire. Includes brief bibliographies of notable personalities of the era, reading lists, and eight pages of photographs.

(#MT511—75¢)

A Short History of 17th Century England: 1603-1689 by *G. E. Aylmer*

A study of the most crucial period in English political history: the struggle between Crown and Parliament during the eighty-six years between the accession to the throne of James I and that of William and Mary. Includes full comparative date chart, maps, and eight pages of photographs.

(#MT512—75¢)

A Short History of 18th Century England: 1689-1793 by *R. W. Harris*

A survey of the forces in England that brought about the triumph of Parliamentary government, the rise of great statesmen, and a growing vitality in commerce and overseas trade that was to make eighteenth-century England into a great world power. Includes bibliography of suggested readings and eight pages of photographs. (#MT515—75¢)

A Short History of 19th Century England: 1793-1868 by *John W. Barry*

A study of England under the impact of the Industrial Revolution, which transformed her from a rural to an urban nation, brought about heated debates on reforms, and posed new questions in areas of politics, philosophy and religion. Includes chronological table of events, comprehensive bibliography and 8 pages of photographs. (#MT516—75¢)

A Short History
of
Twentieth-Century
England

by T. L. JARMAN

A MENTOR BOOK

PUBLISHED BY THE NEW AMERICAN LIBRARY

Published as a MENTOR BOOK
by arrangement with Blandford Press Ltd.,
who have authorized this softcover edition.

First Printing, July, 1963

This book is published in England under the title
Democracy and World Conflict, 1868–1962

MENTOR TRADEMARK REG. U.S. PAT. OFF. AND FOREIGN COUNTRIES
REGISTERED TRADEMARK—MARCA REGISTRADA
HECHO EN CHICAGO, U.S.A.

MENTOR BOOKS are published by
The New American Library of World Literature, Inc.
501 Madison Avenue, New York 22, New York

PRINTED IN THE UNITED STATES OF AMERICA

Contents

List of Illustrations

(Plates will be found between pp. 112-113.)

List of Maps

Acknowledgements

The illustrations have been reproduced by permission of the following:

1, 2, 3, 4, 7, 8, 9 and 10   The Trustees of the National Portrait Gallery

5 and 6   The Radio Times Hulton Picture Library

11, 12, 13, 16, 17 and 18   The Imperial War Museum

14   Karsh of Ottawa

19   The United States Information Service

20   Keystone Press Agency Ltd.

21   Planet News Ltd.

Preface

THE PERIOD OF British history with which this book deals is—especially to those who, like the author, have lived through more than half of it—perhaps the most interesting of all. But it is impossible in writing contemporary history not to be influenced by one's own sympathies, by one's own beliefs, religious, political, and economic. The author has tried to present the facts, but, like every historian, he realizes how elusive facts can be, and how much less susceptible of formulation they are than is generally supposed by the man in the street. At the same time the writer has tried, while giving the facts, to give also something of the colour and feel of great movements and events.

I am grateful to all who have helped me, at home and abroad, either in conversation or by their books. In particular I would like to thank Mr. G. D. Lean for his suggestions on the manuscript as a whole, Professor W. Ashworth for his comments on chapter 4, and Professor H. D. Dickinson for reading and criticising my discussion of economic developments in the final chapter.

My thanks are also due to Miss M. Down and Miss D. O. Terry for typing the manuscript.

T. L. J.

Royal Fort House, Bristol.
September 1962.

The Growth of Democracy

THE YEAR 1868 is a convenient starting point for the study of modern British history. It was the year in which William Ewart Gladstone became Prime Minister for the first time. He brought to his new task a strong religious faith and a belief that God had called him to do His will in politics, and he is still remembered as an outstanding example of a Christian statesman. He really tried to put into practice in his political life the Christian principles which guided his private life. With Gladstone as premier Victorian England was assuming the main characteristics of the picture which older people today can still recall: Christian principle, parliamentary democracy and solid middle-class prosperity.

The death of Palmerston in 1865 had in some ways marked the end of an epoch; he had first held office in Napoleonic times, and had stood for an older, aristocratic order when there was little if any social difference between whigs and tories. But all the time, since the Reform Act of 1832, a new middle-class England had been growing up; industry, capitalism, were its features; free trade triumphed. John Stuart Mill in his essay *On Liberty* defended in classic terms the rights of the individual, above all freedom of thought; Bagehot in *The English Constitution* analysed, explained and justified parliamentary government and the British cabinet system. Only in religion, did Darwin offer a challenge to accepted ideas—and he for the time being was set aside by the bishops.

But although solidity and security may well appear today,

especially to those who remember two world wars, to be the characteristics of the Victorian period, they must not conceal from us that in the years following 1868 we have to trace the origins and development of great changes in our national life—British government was becoming a democracy; popular education was developing; there was the struggle for Irish Home Rule; there was the rise and decline of imperialism; a change was taking place in Britain's economic position relative to that of other countries; and there were the beginnings of socialism and of the Labour Party.

Most important of all, the period of Gladstone's first government saw a profound change in the foreign situation. Prussia's wars of 1864 and 1866 had already brought her victories over Denmark and Austria, and her war of 1870 brought not only victory over France but also the creation of the German Empire. The downfall of France and the emergence of Germany as a Great Power were facts of the first significance. It was said that Europe had lost a mistress and gained a master. No longer could England follow the masterful policy of Palmerston, but moved instead towards "splendid isolation". Eventually the ambitious and restless power in the heart of Europe aroused the fears of its neighbours on either hand, and on two occasions threatened to engulf them. The two world wars of the next century can both be traced back to the rise of modern Germany as a Great Power.

Gladstone and Democracy

When Gladstone first became Prime Minister he was almost fifty-nine, and Queen Victoria was nearly halfway through her long reign. Great Britain was one of the Great Powers of the world, and her people were prosperous—they enjoyed a prosperity to which Gladstone had contributed when as Chancellor of the Exchequer in the governments of Lord Aberdeen, Lord Palmerston and Lord Russell he had swept away tariffs and introduced free trade, bringing increased exports and imports, and had reduced national expenditure and the income tax. As leader of the Liberal Party, he formed a government which was to be responsible for a number of important reforms helping to make the country more democratic. The Reform Acts of 1832 and 1867 had laid the foundations by giving the vote first to the middle class and then to the working class in the towns. On these foundations Gladstone could build. The Act of 1832 had seemed like a revolution at the time. Gladstone himself, then a tory, had thought that reform meant revolution. But there had been no revolution. There was, again, great popular excitement over the second Reform Bill, but all passed off peacefully. Indeed the development of democracy took place very slowly. The young tory Gladstone became in later life the Liberal Leader, and the Conservatives when Gladstone was old might well be more liberal than the Liberals were in his youth.

In 1864 Gladstone had surprised the House of Commons by a speech in which he supported a most important, and to many, a revolutionary, principle.

> I venture to say that every man who is not presumably incapacitated by some consideration of personal unfitness or of political danger, is morally entitled to come within the pale of the Constitution.

In other words, as it seemed to plain men, Gladstone was supporting universal suffrage. Lord Palmerston had been astounded. Liberal Prime Minister as he was then, he was a Liberal of a very different kind from Gladstone. In a letter of rebuke to him, Palmerston declared: "I entirely deny that every sane and not disqualified man has a moral right to vote."

Palmerston belonged to the past, Gladstone to the future. The working men of England, becoming more comfortable, better informed, more steady and reliable, were ready for the vote. Disraeli also realised this, as he showed with his Reform Act of 1867. The Liberals had striven to pass their Reform Bill in 1866, but had failed because of a split in their party—and this in spite of the great efforts of Gladstone who introduced the Bill in the House of Commons to rally the Liberals to the cause of parliamentary reform which was their traditional policy ever since the great Reform Act of 1832. Disraeli had seized his opportunity—he had caught the whigs bathing and stolen their clothes. But one thing Gladstone did for democracy during his first government: in 1872 he passed the Ballot Act which made voting secret. Before this voting had been in public, and some people argued that it was right for the voter to stand up for his opinions in this way. Public voting had meant also, however, that an employer could dismiss a workman if he did not vote as the employer wished. Now this became impossible, and the influence of ordinary people was strengthened.

During his second government Gladstone carried the Third Reform Act, 1884. This extended the male householder and lodger franchise (of 1867) of the boroughs to the countryside also. This extension of the franchise increased the electorate from about three to five millions. In the following year a Redistribution Act introduced the system we know today of single-member constituencies containing approximately the same number of voters. No more important changes were made until after the First World War. The parliamentary Reform Acts had established Britain as a democratic country.

Thus at last voting power was in the hands of the people. Gladstone addressed himself to the masses. Both the Liberal radical, Joseph Chamberlain, and the tory democrat, Lord Randolph Churchill, put forward radical election programmes.[1] It looked as though Chamberlain would follow Gladstone as Prime Minister and bring in a policy of sweeping social reform. But Irish home rule and the Liberal split put an end to this.[2] It was indeed a long time before the masses realised their power. They were not interested in home rule for Ireland. They put into power Lord Salisbury and the Conservatives for nearly twenty years. It was not until the rise of the Labour Party that they felt their power.[3]

In the middle years of the century parliament had been established in its new buildings, which are so familiar today. The old Palace of Westminster, where parliament had

[1] See p. 18 and p. 37.

[2] See Chapter 2, p. 38 and p. 39.

[3] See Chapter 4, p. 81.

formerly met, was destroyed by fire in 1834. Gladstone, first elected in the previous year, used later to recall its poor sanitary arrangements. The massive new buildings in the traditional Gothic style imposed on the onlooker both a sense of the tradition inherent in parliament and a symbol of its majesty and power. At that time there was—before the days of the cinema, wireless and television—a much greater interest and excitement in politics and parliamentary debates. Those who participated have recorded their impression of "the fervour and depth of the political passion of that epoch".

Gladstone and Disraeli: The Liberal and Conservative Parties

For many years Gladstone was faced by a great rival. Gladstone had become leader of the Liberal Party, Disraeli of the Conservative Party. For some sixteen years before 1868 Gladstone and Disraeli had alternated in the course of the party struggle as Chancellors of the Exchequer: now they were to alternate as Prime Ministers. The personal rivalry of these two outstanding men of the century is a marked feature of the political history of the period. Though both were great men, they were very different men. Gladstone came of wealthy Scottish parentage, his father a successful merchant in Liverpool, and went to Eton and Oxford. Endowed with great physical strength, health and energy, he possessed also a powerful mind and a splendid speaking voice. He was profoundly religious, and believed that he was called to do God's work in his political life. He had moved slowly from the toryism in which he was brought up to Liberalism, which experience and religious conviction forced him to embrace. As he said himself, "My toryism was accepted by me on authority and in good faith; I did my best to fight for it. But, on every subject, as I came to deal with it practically, I had to deal with it as a Liberal." He came to be a passionate believer in liberty and justice—which made him the champion of oppressed and downtrodden Ireland. "I was brought up," he said, "to distrust and dislike liberty, I learned to believe in it. That is the key to all my changes." With him as leader, the Liberal Party came to stand for liberty and democratic government, for peace, and for economy and efficiency in government business and finance. "Peace, Retrenchment and Reform" became a Liberal slogan.

As time went on Gladstone became more and more a popular leader. In his speeches he came to appeal to the people, to the masses. At one meeting (in his second Midlothian campaign, 1880) he reckoned up those who were for him and the Liberal Party and those who were against:

I am sorry to say we cannot reckon upon the aristocracy! We cannot reckon upon what is called the landed interest! We cannot reckon upon the clergy of the Established Church! . . . We cannot reckon upon the wealth of the country, nor upon the rank of the country! . . . In the main these powers are against us. . . . But, gentlemen, above all these, and behind all these, there is the nation itself. . . . The nation is a power hard to rouse, but when roused harder still and more hopeless to resist.

Disraeli was a man of a very different kind. Jewish by birth, though baptised into the Church of England, he was never wholly English, and he had to overcome prejudices against his race and his personal peculiarities. He dressed as a dandy in his youth, had not had the conventional public school and university education, travelled a lot abroad, and spent much time and money on pleasure. He was a man of literary genius which showed itself in his novels. That such a man made himself a master of affairs, became leader of the Conservative Party, and twice Prime Minister shows clearly what powerful qualities he possessed behind the façade of affectation which he showed to society. He transformed the Conservative Party from an aristocratic into a popular party. He stood for a tory democracy—he worked for the social improvement of the people, the maintenance of the established institutions of the monarchy and the national church, and above all for the Empire. Imperialism is something inseparably associated with Disraeli.

With Gladstone and Disraeli as leaders, the Liberal and Conservative Parties took firm shape. Differences there were between them as the very names indicate, but the differences must not be exaggerated. There was also much in common; for example, both parties believed strongly in the rights of private property, and it was this strong belief that was eventually to make inevitable the rise of a separate Labour Party to put forward the socialist theory of public rather than private ownership of wealth. But a two-party system was a convenient way of working a democratic system of government; the electors could exercise their choice. Party organisations were built up to further the interests of each party; there was the National Union of Conservative and Constitutional Associations, formed in 1867, and the National Liberal Federation organised in 1877. It came to be a matter of course to think of people everywhere as either Liberals or Conservatives. As the Gilbert and Sullivan opera *Iolanthe* put it in 1882:

> Every boy and every gal
>   That's born into the world alive
> Is either a little Liberal
>   Or else a little Conservative!

But though the Conservative and Liberal Parties are clearly recognisable as two broad groupings of feeling and opinion, neither party was completely homogeneous. Inside each party there were divergent conservative and radical elements. Among the Liberals, Joseph Chamberlain was the radical leader. He had strengthened his power by forming the National Liberal Federation. In September 1885, he campaigned for what was known as the "unauthorised programme", a radical programme startling the whigs, and horrifying the Queen: the radicals wanted free elementary education, graduated taxation (i.e. heavier taxes on the rich to provide money for social reforms), more and stronger local government, and small holdings for agricultural labourers. His breach with Gladstone over home rule stopped any progress in this direction. The Conservative Party found its radical in Lord Randolph Churchill. He and his followers were sometimes known as the "fourth party", and their ideas as "Tory Democracy", in the tradition of Disraeli. Randolph Churchill was a bold and eloquent leader. He favoured social reform, and he based his own power on the popular element, the constituency representatives, in the Conservative central organisation. But he was too headstrong. Chancellor of the Exchequer in Lord Salisbury's second government, he almost at once clashed with his colleagues over his budget proposals. He resigned (end of 1886), thinking the government could not get on without him. But it did—showing, perhaps, thereby how comparatively unimportant was the radical element in a Conservative ministry.

To some extent the allegiance men gave to the political parties was based on local feeling or upon sectional interests and prejudices. Wales was Liberal, and for this there were national and religious reasons. Welsh Nonconformists resented both English domination and the establishment of the Anglican church in Wales, and the struggle to disestablish the church in Wales was thus at the same time a political and a religious struggle. Scotland, too, had its national feelings, not to mention Ireland. Gladstone proposed (1879) for each and for "portions of England" a measure of home rule to relieve Parliament of the growing pressure of business. Those parts of England, mainly the industrial parts, where nonconformity was strong were Liberal. The Liberal Party, though Gladstone himself was a staunch churchman, became more and more the political instrument of Nonconformity. The nonconformists were hostile to the church, supported temperance, and wanted a system of state-supported schools independent of the church instead of the existing church schools. In the south and east of England and in parts of Scotland Conservatism was strong; the Conservatives supported the Church of England, were well disposed to the drink trade, wished to protect the church schools, and were more inclined than the Liberals to support expenditure on the armed services.

For a time the monarchy almost became a pawn in the party strife. After the death of Prince Albert in 1861 Queen Victoria found herself unable to face her public duties without her husband; she retired into herself and lived in seclusion. People felt that the Queen and her family did not earn the large sums of public money expended on their upkeep. By 1871 the Queen was really unpopular. In that year there were demonstrations in Trafalgar Square, an enquiry was asked for in the House of Commons into the Queen's finances, Republican Clubs were founded in many cities, among them Cardiff, Aberdeen and Birmingham, and in the last the radical Liberal, Joseph Chamberlain, spoke as though a republic must eventually be set up in place of the monarchy. Gladstone himself always revered the monarchy as an institution; he was completely loyal to the Queen, never criticised the monarchy in public, and rebuked and held in check the republican feelings of his radical followers. But in trying to bring the Queen out into public life again, Gladstone offended her. He could not flatter her as a woman in the way that Disraeli found so easy. The Queen's dislike for Gladstone and her friendship for Disraeli were factors in the political rivalry of the two leaders, but Gladstone kept to himself the secret that he and the Queen, the two outstanding representatives of the Victorian era, did not act in harmony.

How deep was the Queen's dislike of Gladstone appeared (though not publicly) when she tried to avoid having him as Prime Minister after the great Liberal victory of 1880. The Queen, who was abroad, wrote to her confidential secretary: "She will sooner abdicate than send for or have anything to do with that half-mad fire-brand who would soon ruin everything, and be a Dictator." Meanwhile she was on the best of terms with Disraeli, and expressed her hope that the Conservative Party would soon be in power again.

When the Queen came back more and more into public life, she regained her popularity. As her reign went on her influence grew, and perhaps no monarch has ever made such a great and enduring impression. She has given her name to the age. Yet her actual power in the system of government did not increase. Instead parliament and people were extending and consolidating their power as political and social reform opened doors to talent and widened the opportunity for a better life.

Liberal Reforms: Gladstone's First Government

When he headed his first government in 1868, Gladstone

was devoting his attention to, above all, the Irish problem. But other members of his government were interested in social reforms of various kinds: Cardwell, the Secretary of War, for example, was aiming at army reform, and W. E. Forster, a prosperous West Riding woollen manufacturer who had married a daughter of Dr Thomas Arnold, the headmaster of Rugby School, was in charge of education. Indeed the Liberal government of 1868 was a great reforming government—its reforms followed the extension of the franchise in 1867 (by Disraeli), just as a series of important reforms had followed the first great extension by the Reform Act of 1832.

The reforms of Gladstone's government were democratic in character; they opened doors of opportunity to people who had previously been shut out, in one way or another, from careers in the public service, the universities or the army. At the same time such reforms did something to improve the efficiency of government and public affairs. Up to this time men who worked for the government as its paid officials obtained their posts, not because they were well qualified to hold them, but because they were relations, friends, or connections of ministers or of their important political supporters. Now by an Order in Council of 1870, Gladstone opened entry to most branches of the Civil Service (except the foreign office) to open competition. Young men with ability and good education could pass an examination, and enter upon a career in the public service. Another sphere in which there were great obstacles to talent was that of the universities. Careers as teachers or students at Oxford and Cambridge, in the colleges and in the universities themselves, had been open only to members of the Church of England. By the University Tests Act of 1871 these teaching posts were thrown open to men of all creeds.

The army also greatly needed reform. The soldiers came from the poorest and least educated sections of the population. The officers came from the upper classes, but they were amateurs. They served in the army, but looked upon it as a kind of sport, which they might follow for a time, like hunting or social life. This might be well enough when what chiefly counted in war was courage and physical strength, spirit and dash. But it was not enough when soldiering became a skilled job, and when an officer needed education and technical training. The Crimean War had revealed the great defects in the organisation behind the British army; the Franco-Prussian war showed what an efficient army was like. The victories of the German army did something to alarm British opinion, and create a climate in which reform of the army was possible. An anonymous magazine article, *The Battle of Dorking,* had a great success with its imaginary picture of a German invasion of Britain.

Cardwell, who was a very able man, devoted the best part of his active political life to army reforms, and he carried them through partly by Acts of Parliament, partly by administrative measures. He exhausted himself in the process, as there was great opposition from the Conservatives, the House of Lords, and from most army officers. Gentlemen and sportsmen, they thought they could get on as Marlborough's and Wellington's officers had done, without specialised military training.

Cardwell strengthened the position of the Secretary for War, making the commander-in-chief subordinate to him. Previously there had been rivalry between the commander-in-chief and a number of departments, now the Secretary for War was put in supreme control. He abolished flogging in the army during peacetime—and this, though it was opposed by most senior officers, was an important part of his policy of raising the status of the soldier. The harsh and brutal conditions of army life—long service enlistment and flogging—had made the army a kind of penal servitude. Men enlisted for twelve years—the most active years of their lives—and when they were eventually discharged they were untrained and unfitted for civilian employment. Most soldiers served a large part of their service in India or elsewhere in unhealthy conditions, and this lowered their physique. The army in war needed younger men, and men in full vigour. Such were the reasons why Cardwell introduced a system of short service. Men would henceforth serve six years actually in the army, followed by six years in the reserve. He also reorganised the army on a new basis. The old infantry regiments which were known by numbers had a long history and a certain corporate spirit, but Cardwell found it better to re-arrange them on a county basis. Each regiment was given the name of a county or other area, and was to contain at least two battalions. One battalion would serve abroad, while the other would remain at the county depot and be a centre for recruitment and training. The regimental depot would also make a link with the auxiliary forces, militia and vol-unteers, which were based on the county.

Perhaps the most important, and certainly the best remem-bered of Cardwell's reforms was the abolition in 1871 of the practice of purchasing commissions. An officer's commission was not bought, as might be thought, from the government or the army, but a young man bought a commission from an officer who wished to leave the army and sold it again when he himself was ready to leave. A commission had become, in-deed, a form of private property. Although promotion could come in wartime directly, if a higher-ranking officer were killed, to be an officer depended in peacetime not upon ability and efficiency, but upon having enough money to pur-chase the commission, and promotion, too, depended also upon purchase. The system of purchase had been supported by Wellington, and was still stoutly defended by leading soldiers. Their argument was that it enabled older officers to retire—the sale of the commission helped them like a pen-sion—and so younger officers, stronger physically, gained promotion. A stream of young officers through the Service was maintained. But it certainly prevented any proper method of selecting and promoting officers by merit. The Liberals, at-tacking privilege, made good use of the case of Lord Cardigan. This notorious officer, who died in 1868, had bought his way to command, had used his position to enjoy himself, and had been forced to leave the service because of his abominable treatment of officers and men under him. But undismayed he had bought himself the command of another regiment. Brave—he had led the charge of the Light Brigade in the Crimea—he was nevertheless a bully, and unfit for command. How, by means of his wealth he had twice secured it, was a striking, if extreme, example of what could take place under the purchase system. It took, however, all Cardwell's efforts along with the personal intervention of

Gladstone to secure abolition of purchase. Their success improved the efficiency of the army—but not only this; it was in line with reform of the Civil Service in opening careers to men of ability who might not have wealth and family influence behind them.

Another very important measure was the Education Act of 1870. Education, in the sense of a system organised to provide it for all, was almost a new idea in England. That this should have been the case, is hard to realise today. Now that everyone goes to school it takes an effort of historical imagination to recall a time when schools were few and poor, and run largely by the religious initiative of the churches. There were the public schools and the universities of Oxford and Cambridge for the few: to provide churchmen, scholars and a handful of men with a smattering of knowledge and culture. For other people there were private schools to teach reading and writing, if these skills were needed, and sometimes special schools or colleges, as for lawyers and doctors. Beyond this, craftsmen, merchants and shopkeepers, and business people learned through apprenticeship, they were trained by working for masters in their particular trade. But with the industrial revolution, population increased fast. There were many more children who needed some kind of training, and who could not be left in complete ignorance. The Church of England and the Nonconformists began to set up elementary schools, to give elementary instruction, that is, in reading, writing and arithmetic, and also to teach children to read the Bible and to give them some idea of good conduct and moral behaviour. Both Church of England and Nonconformists wished to give the children what they felt was most important—their own denominational religious beliefs. They wanted state aid for themselves, but not for other schools. It was therefore difficult to create a state system of elementary education. Yet the need for it was growing and becoming clearer. England had to face competition from other countries. Some of them, Germany for example, had already much better schools. Prussian victories in war, too, seemed to speak well for the German system of education. In addition, English workmen had the vote

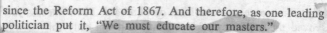

since the Reform Act of 1867. And therefore, as one leading politician put it, "We must educate our masters."

Forster's Education Act laid the foundation of a national system of education, for it made provision for elementary schools at public expense. The Act divided the country into school districts, based on the boroughs and parishes. It did not replace the church schools, where these existed and where sufficient. But if there were no church schools or they were insufficient for the task, then the ratepayers were to elect a School Board which was to set up schools. These new schools would be paid for partly by grants from the government and partly out of the local rates, while the existing church schools would continue to be aided by the government.

Later on, of course, further Acts of Parliament extended elementary education. In 1880 education was made compulsory for all children under twelve, and in 1891 it was made free. These were most important steps forward, for like the opening of the Civil Service, the universities, and like army reform, they opened the door of opportunity. At last there were schools for all; children could acquire the basic educational skills and the rudiments of knowledge. The development of industrial Britain was making it essential for all to have a minimum of education. People could hardly, any longer, live and work effectively without it. Experience showed, as time went on, how important a system of education is; every country, as it has developed, has found itself in need of one. Schools, it has been found, are not a luxury but a necessity.

The Liberal government had made many changes—important and mostly for the good. But at last people got tired of it, and were ready for a rest after so many reforms carried out and so much excitement over them. People were not enthusiastic about elementary education; the Licensing Act of 1872, a moderate temperance measure to limit public house hours of opening, alienated powerful brewing interests; the trade union legislation of 1871 had not won working-class support. Gladstone, the great Liberal theorist, did not well understand the material needs of working people. He had strengthened the position of trade unions in giving legal recognition but did *not* legalise peaceful picketing, without which strikes were ineffective. This left a way open for Disraeli, a little later on, to win working-class support. Disraeli mocked the Liberal ministers, comparing them with "exhausted volcanoes". The election of 1874 brought the Conservatives into power, although Gladstone had proposed to abolish income tax, a financial reform which interested him far more than trade unionism. Disraeli became Prime Minister.

Disraeli's Government

Thus, at last, Disraeli had his chance.[5] Once before he had been Prime Minister for a few months; this time he had a safe majority behind him. But now Disraeli was old—he was seventy—and his devoted wife had died a short time before. He was a lonely man. Nevertheless his ministry was in many ways a memorable one. Monarchy and Empire were cardinal points in his political creed. Nor had Disraeli forgotten social reform which, according to the ideal he had expressed in his novels nearly thirty years before, should bridge the gap between rich and poor. His was a bold, new attitude in face of the prevailing ideas of *laissez faire*, and an early pointer towards the welfare state. He appointed Richard Cross as Home Secretary, and Cross, a successful Lancashire lawyer and banker, brought his knowledge of practical affairs to bear in the working out of Conservative social reform. In 1875 the Public Health Act improved sanitary regulations. Town councils were to appoint a medical officer of health to fight infectious diseases and see to the proper maintenance of the sewers. In the same year the Artisans' Dwellings Act empowered the councils of the larger towns to pull down slums and replace them with decent buildings. The supply of clean water, parks and recreation grounds was encouraged. The Enclosure of Commons Act, in the following year, prevented landowners from absorbing into their estates what remained of the old common lands. Then, in 1878, Cross codified, in

[5] For Disraeli as Conservative leader, see p. 16; for Disraeli and Imperialism, see pp. 46–50; for Disraeli and the social problem, see p. 78.

his Factories and Workshops Act, the factory legislation which had been growing in extent and complexity ever since the first Factory Act of 1833. Thus the laws controlling hours and conditions of work were made clearer and more consistent.

Then there was an important law to help trade unions. The Conspiracy and Protection of Property Act of 1875 fixed the vital principle that a union could not be prosecuted for an act which would be legal if done by an individual. Since it was not illegal for an individual man to stop working, it followed that a union could not be prosecuted for conspiracy if it organised a strike. "Peaceful picketing" was also to be allowed, meaning that a union could place men outside a factory during a strike to persuade their fellows not to go in and work.

Later Political Changes

At the General Election of 1880 the political pendulum swung again. Disraeli's government was defeated, and Gladstone came back to head his second government. The successive changes of government, from one party to the other, which seemed to surprise people at the time, have often been described as "the swing of the pendulum" for they show the two-party system in operation—a marked feature of British parliamentary democracy.

Another important measure, the Local Government Act of 1888, was carried by the Conservative government of Lord Salisbury which was in power from 1886 to 1892. This Act brought self-government to the countryside. Previously (though the towns had had elected councils since the Whig Municipal Reform Act of 1835) the country districts had been governed by the Justices of the Peace, who were nominated from above, not elected. By the new Act County Councils were to be elected by the ratepayers, and these councils would replace the J.P.'s in the management of drains, roads and bridges, and share with them the control of the police. The Liberals in 1894 extended the network of democratically elected councils, by establishing urban and rural district councils, and parish councils—all subordinate to the county councils. Thus in the ordinary workaday affairs of local government as well as in the making of the laws at Westminster the people of Britain were coming to take an ever increasing share.

Evolution of Democracy

2

The Struggle for Irish Home Rule

M Y MISSION," said Gladstone on the eve of becoming Prime Minister in 1868, "is to pacify Ireland." When he spoke these words he was taking one of his favourite forms of exercise, cutting down trees in his park at Hawarden. He did not speak again until the tree was down. Ireland had long been on his mind, although he had never visited Ireland and had little real knowledge of the country's problems. Such ignorance was common among members of his government and the British people generally. Gladstone did go later on to Ireland, for three weeks in 1877; Disraeli never visited it. But Gladstone had never forgotten the conversation he had had during a visit to Paris as long ago as 1845, with the French historian Guizot. Guizot had impressed upon him the bad view which many foreigners took of the English treatment of Ireland. Disraeli did not think that Gladstone would get far with Ireland as a political policy—English hatred of popery and of the Irish would be too strong for him. But Disraeli had not understood how deep was Gladstone's hatred of injustice and how strong his determination to do the right.

Ireland's Wrongs

Ireland in the past had been deeply wronged. There was grave discontent. Indeed Ireland inherited a historic legacy of hatred, which went back to the bitter wars of Tudor and

28

Stuart times, to the crushing of rebellion by Cromwell, and to the terrible sufferings of the potato famine of 1846–7, when the Irish were reported to be dying at the rate of 15,000 a day. The horrors of the potato famine left indelible impressions on Irish minds, of the Irish roads littered with starved and dying people, and of emigrant ships to America on which sometimes three-quarters of the Irish would die before the ship reached New York. By 1851 the population of Ireland was reduced by over one and a half millions. The Act of Union of 1800 had joined Ireland to Great Britain, and brought Irish members to parliament (although until catholic emancipation in 1829 protestants only could sit in parliament), but deep-rooted problems remained. For these problems were rooted not only in Ireland's historic past, but also in the fundamental character of the country: Ireland was Celtic and Roman Catholic. The Celtic, catholic peasants were burdened, as a result of the conquests, with English protestant landlords. These landlords, many of them, lived in England and took little interest in their Irish estates apart from the rents they drew from them; the tenants, therefore, had to pay high rents, and were evicted if they did not pay. The Irish peasants were very poor, not much above the starvation level. In their midst, also, there was an alien church established, the Church of England.

Disraeli summarised all this in what was almost a definition of the Irish problem:

> A dense population in extreme distress inhabit an island where there is an Established church which is not their church, and a territorial aristocracy, the richest of whom live in a distant capital. Thus they have a starving population, an absentee aristocracy, an alien church, and in addition the weakest Executive in the world.

Gladstone's Early Measures

Gladstone first of all dealt with the problem of the Church of England in Ireland. During the General Election preceding his first government, he compared the ascendancy of the Protestant Church of England in Roman Catholic Ireland with:

some tall tree of noxious growth, lifting its head to Heaven and poisoning the atmosphere of the land as far as its shadow can extend. It is still there, gentlemen, but now at last the day has come when, as we hope, the axe has been laid to the root (loud cheers). . . . There lacks, gentlemen, but one stroke more—the stroke of these Elections (loud cheers). It will then, once for all, topple to its fall, and on that day the heart of Ireland will leap for joy, and the mind and conscience of England and Scotland will repose with thankful satisfaction upon the thought that something has been done towards the discharge of national duty, and towards deepening and widening the foundations of public strength, security and peace. (Loud and prolonged applause.)

Once Prime Minister, Gladstone tackled the problem. The axe was indeed laid to the root. He had to admit that his attack on the Church of England in Ireland represented a change of view in himself. A devout Anglican, he had thirty years before in a book on *Church and State* supported the closest union between state and Church of England. Now he saw that, in Ireland, this could not be.

In spite of all opposition—for the Queen disliked his Irish policy seeing in it only a means of rallying the Liberal Party and in Ireland he was denounced by protestants as an enemy of God—Gladstone carried in 1869 his Act for the Disestablishment of the Church in Ireland. The tree was down.

The established state church in Ireland was transformed into a self-governing corporation; the Irish bishops ceased to be appointed by the Crown and ceased to sit in the House of Lords. At the same time the Irish church was disendowed. Tithes had been converted by an Act of 1838 into a rent-charge payable by the landlord, not the tenant, and an arrangement was now made for landlords to extinguish these charges at the end of forty-five years. The Act also enabled tenants of church estates to buy their holdings with financial help from the state. Church property, estimated at £16,-000,000, was divided so as to pay the stipends and retirement annuities of the existing clergy, and to provide a fund (about £7,350,000) for the relief of calamity and suffering. Bold as the Act was, however, it was not what was needed to pacify Ireland—it was the land, not the destruction of the alien church, which was the crucial issue, as an Irish bishop pointed out in the debate in the House of Lords. Lord Cairns, a great Irish lawyer, made the same point: "The Roman Catholic population of Ireland merely look upon the destruction of the Establishment as a preliminary to the destruction of the landlords."

Meanwhile Gladstone was considering two plans to bring the Royal Family into closer association with Ireland. He thought the Queen should have a royal residence there, and pay visits to it as she did to her beloved Balmoral in Scotland. Secondly, the Prince of Wales might be made Viceroy of Ireland. These plans were not merely part of an Irish policy; they were also an instrument of Gladstone's endeavour to bring the Queen back into public life, and to do something to counteract the unpopularity of the monarchy at the time. But the Queen did not welcome these proposals, and they came to nothing.

More difficult than the problem of church disestablishment, was the problem of the Irish land and the poverty of its tenants. To this matter Gladstone turned next. After studying the problem Gladstone was convinced that tenants in Ireland had been reduced to their sorry position as a result of conquests and confiscations which had put them at the mercy of their English landlords. The law in Ireland was not different from the law in England, but the social relationship between landlord and tenant was very different. What was happening in Ireland was, perhaps, more like what had been happening in England a century earlier during the enclosures. In England, tenant-farmers were often substantial men, and there was a closely knit community feeling among the landlord or squire, the parson, and the tenant-farmers. Rights of property were freely admitted and recognised. But in Ireland the tenant was little better than a labourer, and his landlord would dispense with him and evict him at will. To these Irish tenants it seemed that the landlord's right of property was founded in wrong. The most tangible and immediate grievances were the landlord's right to raise rents and ignore the improvements which might have been put into a landholding by a tenant's hard work and ingenuity.

Gladstone, therefore, passed an Irish Land Act in 1870 to protect tenants from unfair treatment. The Act forced landlords to pay compensation to tenants if they were evicted (for any cause other than not paying the rent), and fixed a scale of compensation to cover improvements and also disturbance caused in having to move. The Act, indeed, did something to help overburdened tenants. Gladstone thought, at the moment, that he had solved the Irish land problem, but the new law did not go far enough to protect the Irish against too high rents. The Act did not, therefore, work very well. By 1875 a great agricultural depression was setting in, and many Irish tenants could not pay their rents. New measures became necessary.

Demand for Irish Home Rule: Parnell

Meanwhile, however, and during Disraeli's government (1874–80) agitation developed in Ireland for home rule. At first this was a peaceful, constitutional movement, launched by Isaac Butt, formerly a professor at Trinity College, Dublin, in 1870. As leader of 59 Irish members in the House of Commons Butt put his case in a reasonable and friendly way, yet, as has happened so often, the moderate man was rebuffed, and, as a consequence, the leadership passed into the hands of extremists. In 1878 Butt resigned, and a little later Charles Stewart Parnell took his place. Parnell was a young Irish landlord, and although he was a protestant (like Butt), he had acquired anti-English feelings from his American mother. He proved himself an astute and resolute leader, with a powerful personality which impressed itself on the political life of the day. He had quickly seen the possibilities of the Ballot Act. Before it, the Irish voters had been easily intimidated; under the direction of their landlords they had elected members to the two existing English parties. After the secret ballot, there could be an independent Irish Party. Parnell, as leader of this party, soon made himself master of a new parliamentary tactic—obstruction. By keeping the House of Commons up all night with their speeches, the Irish could hold up the progress of all business. This was a new and sensational method of forcing the Irish Party and its problems on the attention of the British parliament.

In Ireland itself, the agrarian problem became acute with the agricultural slump which set in after 1875. Direct action began, and the Fenians, an older organisation believing in physical force, began to take a hand. In 1879 the Irish Land League was formed, with Parnell as president, and with Fenians as secretary and treasurer. Financial support came in from America. The League's object was to agitate for reduction of rents, and ultimately for the state to buy out landlords and to establish peasant proprietorship. Thus, there was a double Irish attack—in Ireland itself, scattered over the countryside, and in England in the House of Commons. The Irish problem was becoming a major challenge to British statesmanship.

During Gladstone's second government (1880–5) the Irish question was dominant. Ireland was the scene of misery and disorder. Evictions were widespread, and they led to agrarian outrages in retaliation. In 1877 there had been 2,177 evictions and 236 outrages; by 1880 the figures had risen to 10,457 evictions and 2,590 outrages. Ricks were set on fire, cattle were maimed, and gangs went round at night shooting into houses and attacking people. Sometimes there was murder. And once again Parnell hit on a new method of attack—if a new tenant took over a farm from one who had been evicted, he should be "isolated from his kind as if he were a leper of old". From the first person to be treated in this way, a landlord's agent called Captain Boycott, came the name which has ever since been given to this kind of treatment. The policy was successful; it gave the authorities great trouble. A prosecution was instigated against Parnell and the Land League for conspiracy, but the jury failed to agree. Then the government introduced a Coercion Bill into the House of Commons. The Irish launched a fury of obstruction against it, and most of the Irish members were suspended. But the Bill passed in March 1881, and gave the authorities in Ireland special powers of arrest.

Gladstone had also a measure of another kind ready. He passed his second Irish Land Act, in August 1881. It gave what were known as the "three Fs"—fixity of tenure, fair rents and free sale. This meant that leases were to be for fifteen years and were to be renewable; a Land Commission was set up to fix fair rents; and a tenant on leaving his holding could sell his interest (his improvements) to the in-coming tenant. The Act did eventually bring a degree of peace to the Irish countryside; evictions were greatly reduced in number, and with them the number of outrages.

Parnell, however, had observed that violence appeared to be winning greater concessions than had ever been won in the old days of Butt's conciliatory methods and so he went on fighting. He made himself such a nuisance both in the House of Commons and in agitating in Ireland to persuade the people not to drop their anti-English activity, that at length he was arrested and imprisoned in Kilmainham Gaol, situated in a Dublin suburb of that name.

Parnell was in prison nearly six months (October 1881–April 1882), but coercion did not quell the agitation. Indeed, while it lasted, outrages increased, as did also the number of persons killed. Both the British government and Parnell were at length prepared to feel their way towards a settlement. An arrangement was fixed up—the so-called Kilmainham Treaty—by which Parnell and other Irish leaders were released on condition that they used their influence to bring crimes and disorder to an end. For a moment, the prospect looked brighter. With the failure of the coercion policy, the viceroy and chief secretary (W. E. Forster, who had won fame with his Education Act) resigned. But in May 1882 the new chief secretary, Lord Frederick Cavendish, was murdered in Phoenix Park, Dublin, along with Mr Burke, the under-secretary, who was the real object of the attack. The two men were done to death with knives at the hands of a gang (the members of which were later arrested, five being hanged). The murder aroused horror. Parnell himself was shaken—he feared that he might himself be struck down by some secret society (he was said to carry a revolver in his pocket). But in spite of the horror at the murder and new attempts of the government to repress crime in Ireland, things did quieten for a time. The Land Act of 1881 helped a temporary appeasement.

Parnell presently found himself in a position to bargain

with each of the English parties. His objective was home rule for Ireland, and the support his Irish Party could give to either the Conservative or Liberal Party became a major factor in British politics. As the liberal government began to weaken—there had from its beginning been a rift between the whigs and the radicals and the loss of General Gordon at Khartoum in 1885 spelt its doom—the Conservatives angled for Irish support by an approach to Parnell. When with his help the Liberal government was defeated in parliament in the summer of 1885, Lord Salisbury became Prime Minister. The Conservatives naturally wished to retain Irish support. To do this, they modified the coercive measures of the government in Ireland, and passed an Act (Lord Ashbourne's) to give state assistance to Irish tenants who wished to buy their holdings. Thus the Conservatives advanced Parnell's policy of peasant ownership of land in Ireland, a policy towards which the Liberals had also moved. The new viceroy of Ireland, Lord Carnarvon, a former colonial secretary who had sponsored the Act of 1867 which federated Canada and had favoured federation for South Africa, now thought that it was feasible to give Ireland a degree of home rule like that of a province inside the Dominion of Canada. Lord Salisbury allowed Carnarvon to open secret negotiations with Parnell. Parnell was ready—he did not mind which English party enabled him to get home rule so long as he got it, and the Conservatives even had, for him, an advantage over the Liberals in that they had the preponderant voice in the House of Lords.

Meanwhile Gladstone himself had reached the conclusion that home rule must come, although he kept his decision unknown to his colleagues. He had always sympathised with the cause of nationalism, in Italy and in the Balkans. Now Ireland offered a similar challenge at home. Nationalism for Gladstone was a matter of principle, it represented for him an ideal of self-respect, independence, and manhood. It was during a holiday (August 1885) in the Norwegian fiords that Gladstone made up his mind to work for home rule. He saw the Norwegians, the inhabitants of a small country, living happily in their democratic way. Why should not the Irish live in the same way?

But Gladstone, at first, was not anxious to take the lead in this matter. He saw the danger of Ireland becoming a plaything, a bargaining counter in the struggle between the English parties. The process of bidding, between the two parties, for the Irish vote was distasteful to him. He knew it would be difficult to win over all his Liberal followers to the new policy. His own popularity had declined, he was getting old, it was a big job to undertake a fight for home rule. Perhaps, he thought, it might be possible for a Conservative leader to introduce home rule, and to receive Liberal backing if necessary; he thought of the precedents, cases where Liberal reforms had been carried by the Conservatives: there was Disraeli's Reform Act of 1867, and earlier examples, the repeal of the Corn Laws in 1846 and catholic emancipation in 1829. Thus Gladstone could not show his hand, for if it became known that home rule was to be the Liberal policy then Lord Salisbury could not carry his own party with him in supporting it. Parnell tried to find out what Gladstone would offer, what kind and degree of home rule, but Gladstone kept his own counsel. So Parnell made some kind of a bargain with the Conservatives. Just before the elections began in November 1885, Parnell ordered the Irish people living in England to vote Conservative.

In spite of Parnell's action, the elections resulted in a Liberal victory, a majority of 86 over the Conservatives. But the Irish Party had just that number of members. Parnell was now the arbiter in parliament: he could decide the lot of either party. Gladstone still hoped that the Conservatives would, with Irish support, take up and settle the matter of home rule. But the secret of Gladstone's conversion to home rule leaked out, and with this news in the newspapers his hope was doomed to disappointment. The parties began once more to fight on party lines: the Conservatives to defend the Union of Great Britain and Ireland, the Liberals to press for home rule. So it came about that when the Conservatives were defeated in the House of Commons in January, the Liberals came back to office. In February 1886, Gladstone formed his third government.

Gladstone's First Home Rule Bill

The Liberal leader was faced with a task of immense difficulty. He had to persuade his colleagues in the party and his followers at large that home rule was the right policy. There was in the country no especial love for the Irish. Parnell's hatred of England had done nothing to improve the situation. The outrages in Ireland, the shooting and murders and maiming of animals, had made English opinion still more unfavourable to placing Ireland in the hands of Parnell and his party. Some of Gladstone's most powerful colleagues were against home rule; they were irritated and angry because their leader had not taken them into his confidence before the issue was forced upon them, and they doubted the wisdom and practicability of trusting Ireland to govern herself. They disliked, also, a step which would appear to reduce the power of England and weaken her overseas links at a time when the Empire idea was more and more influencing the British imagination.

Gladstone had difficulty in forming his government. Leading members of his earlier governments refused to join him, the most notable being the whig Lord Hartington. When the Home Rule Bill was discussed in the cabinet, the leading radical, Joseph Chamberlain, as well as some minor ministers resigned. Thus there were defections on both the right and left wings of the Liberal Party. The veteran, John Bright, also condemned home rule. Particularly important was the loss of Chamberlain, the successful Birmingham manufacturer, with his strong radical appeal to the masses. It was he who, only three years earlier, had attacked Lord Salisbury and his followers as "the class . . . who toil not neither do they spin" and who had swung the countryside behind the Liberals in the recent elections by his advanced agricultural policy of "three acres and a cow" for each labourer. He thought his social policy more important than any struggle for Irish home rule.

But Gladstone persevered. On April 8th he introduced the Home Rule Bill in a powerful speech which lasted three and a half hours. He maintained that it was the duty of parliament to find an answer "to the question whether it is or is not possible to establish good and harmonious relations between Great Britain and Ireland on the footing of those free institutions to which Englishmen, Scotchmen and Irishmen are alike unalterably attached". He argued that the British, with their firm attachment to free institutions, would not be willing to coerce the Irish indefinitely, and that the result of their efforts at coercion had so far made matters worse:

> What are the results that have been produced? This result above all—and now I come to what I consider to be the basis of the whole mischief—that rightly or wrongly, yet in point of fact, law is discredited in Ireland, and discredited in Ireland upon this ground especially—that it comes to the people of that country with a foreign aspect, and in a foreign garb.

To put that right it was necessary that the Irish should have the responsibility of making their own laws. What then of the Union, the Union of Great Britain and Ireland? The problem, he said, was "how to reconcile Imperial unity with diversity of legislation." To solve this problem, he said, there must be a legislative body, sitting in Dublin, for the conduct of Irish affairs while imperial affairs would remain the concern of the parliament and government in Great Britain.

In bringing this long speech to a close, Gladstone asked the House to accept a measure which would strengthen the British parliament by freeing it from the hostility and obstruction of the Irish members and at the same time save the country the great cost of governing Ireland against its will. He appealed also on the widest ground of principle:

> I ask you to show to Europe and to America that we, too, can face political problems which America twenty years ago faced, and which many countries in Europe have been called upon to face, and have not feared to deal with. (He had mentioned as examples the union of Norway and Sweden and the dual monarchy of Austria–Hungary.) I ask that in our own case we should practise, with firm and fearless hand, what we have so often preached—that the concession of local self-government is not the way to sap or impair, but the way to strengthen and consolidate unity. I ask that

we should apply to Ireland that happy experience which we gained in England and in Scotland . . . that the best and surest foundation we can find to build upon is the foundation afforded by the affections, the convictions, and the will of the nation; and it is thus, by the decree of the Almighty, that we may be enabled to secure at once the social peace, the fame, the power and the permanence of the Empire.

The Home Rule Bill proposed, in short, an Irish parliament and executive in Dublin, with certain subjects reserved for the British government, namely the relation to the crown, peace and war, defence, foreign relations, customs and excise, trade, post office and coinage. The representation of Ireland by members in the British parliament was to be brought to an end, which would free Westminster from Irish obstructionism and mean that Irish Nationalists would never again hold the balance between British parties. In addition, a separate Bill was to provide for further purchase of land by Irish tenants with the aid of loans; this would not only have helped the Irish but would also have helped the English landlords to sell out their interests in Ireland and so escape any hard measures the Irish parliament might take against them.

The Bill was debated in the House of Commons gravely and seriously on sixteen days. But it was rejected. Members had no special love for the Irish Party, and disliked the idea of its being able to dictate its own will. Lord Randolph Churchill began to attack the injustice of protestant Ulster being submerged in a Roman Catholic Ireland; "Ulster will fight, and Ulster will be right!" was a slogan he voiced with damaging effect. In any case, the split in the Liberal Party was fatal to the Bill. Lord Hartington would not desert the English landlords in Ireland, and Joseph Chamberlain declared himself a Liberal Unionist. Both these men were powerful debaters, and their speeches in parliament had great effect. The defeat of the Bill came on June 8th, 1886, by 343 votes to 313, with 93 Liberals voting against the Bill.

The Conservatives and Ireland

Gladstone did not resign, but carried the struggle to the

country in elections. But the elections proved that the country, very much more than parliament, was against home rule. The Liberals suffered a heavy defeat, and Lord Salisbury became Prime Minister. Even now Gladstone did not despair. He thought that if the Irish persevered for a few years more, working constitutionally and by peaceful means, using persistent and free discussion, then eventually opposition would crumble away, and the Nationalists would achieve their aim of home rule. Gladstone could not foresee that the Liberals were—with the exception of those years when home rule was to have a second chance—to be out of office for many years. In the struggle for Irish home rule the Liberal Party had split, and in so doing handed the future to the Conservatives. But had Gladstone succeeded how different the future might have been. The Irish at that time would have been satisfied with what he offered, and the healing influence of time might have led to a permanent reconciliation and avoided the bloody struggle of later years.

From 1886 onwards until 1892 Salisbury's second government, supported by the Liberal Unionists under Hartington and Chamberlain, ruled Ireland strongly and sternly. Renewed coercive measures, in a new Crimes Act, were administered by A. J. Balfour, Lord Salisbury's nephew, who showed courage and determination in enforcing the law and who, in parliamentary debate, could stand up to Gladstone. For there were troubles again in Ireland. Renewed evictions led to the "Plan of Campaign", circulated throughout the country and calling on tenants to organise on each estate and negotiate as a body with the landlord. If the landlord did not accept their offer of rent, it was to be paid into a campaign fund. The leaders of the campaign were new men, and the movement was not the work of Parnell. He was now realising, as Gladstone had hoped, the need to win over British opinion by avoiding extremist acts in Ireland. But he could not hold back his own extremists. Disorders and outrages were followed by repression at the hands of the English authorities. In September 1887, a demonstration at Mitchelstown, in County Cork, led to the police opening fire which caused several deaths. Gladstone himself framed the slogan "Remember Mitchelstown" which for a long time was used by supporters of home rule in each country. Not only this, but a large radical demonstration to support the Irish struggle was staged in Trafalgar Square on November 13th, and was long remembered as "Bloody Sunday". Troops were called to clear the square; though there was no firing, many people were hurt, police as well as civilians, and two civilians died of their injuries.

During the same year *The Times* published in facsimile a letter, ascribed to Parnell, approving the Phoenix Park murders. Parnell denounced this letter as a forgery, and after a long government investigation it was shown that Parnell was right. The letter was found indeed to be a forgery, a clever one which had deceived *The Times*. The forger fled abroad, and shot himself. These events brought a swing of British opinion in favour of Parnell and towards a more favourable view of his cause. Parnell's fortunes and those of his party rose again, but in 1890 the sudden disclosure of the secret in his private life ruined both him and the movement which he led. Captain O'Shea gained a divorce from his wife, the co-respondent being Parnell. Little blame in fact attached to Parnell—O'Shea was a spendthrift and had been for many years virtually separated from his wife, who had formed a genuine, though of course illicit, union with Parnell—but the general public was quite unprepared for the revelation which in those days was thought profoundly shocking. The Irish Party at first supported Parnell, but the Liberal Party— mainly motivated by the Nonconformist conscience—were unwilling to associate with the Irish Party unless it changed its leader. Over this matter, the Irish Party split; those who followed Parnell struggled desperately to maintain their position as an independent party, those who opposed Parnell remained attached to alliance with the Liberals. Next year Parnell married Mrs O'Shea, but his health had been weakened by his incessant political campaigning and his married life was short. After addressing an open-air meeting in the rain he became seriously ill, and returned to his wife at Brighton to die on October 6th. But although in Ireland there was nation-wide mourning, the death of the powerful and brilliant leader did not settle the political difficulties of the Irish Party. There was no reconciliation among the Irish Party members, who continued to quarrel among themselves. Meanwhile Balfour had secured a fair measure of order in Ireland, and introduced some constructive measures. By his Land Act in 1891 he created the Congested Districts Board with funds to help farmers in areas where holdings were uneconomic, by enabling them to increase the size of their holdings and by providing cheap seed and agricultural information. Sea-fishing was also encouraged by providing boats and piers.

The Conservatives, indeed, can claim to have done much for Ireland; though they refused home rule, they passed measures which gave solid economic advantages. Lord Ashbourne's Land Act of 1885 was an unpretentious but effective beginning of land purchase for Irish peasants. Balfour's measure of 1891 helped further. Local government on the basis of election was applied in Ireland in 1898, and a department for agriculture, industries and technical instruction was set up. Later, Balfour's government passed the Irish Land Purchase Act in 1903. This at last put an end to the agrarian problem: the government lent £100,000,000 to the Irish peasants to buy out their landlords. But these last measures were still in the future.

Gladstone's Second Home Rule Bill

The election of 1892 brought the Liberals back to the House with a small majority—there were 273 Liberals and 81 Irish members against 269 Conservatives and 46 Liberal Unionists. The Conservative government did not resign before parliament met, but was defeated on a vote of No Confidence, proposed by H. H. Asquith. The new Liberal government, dependent upon Irish support, had an unsure position. But it contained some able men, among them three future prime ministers, Lord Rosebery, Campbell-Bannerman and Asquith. It was Gladstone's fourth ministry, and he was nearly eighty-three, but the vigorous old man was determined to do his duty as he saw it, to settle, if he could, the Irish problem.

The new Home Rule Bill, which Gladstone introduced in February 1893, was similar to the Bill of 1886. The chief difference was that, in addition to the Irish parliament in Dublin, 80 Irish members were to sit at Westminster to vote only on imperial or Irish affairs. In his opening speech Gladstone spoke for two and a half hours. Once more the Prime Minister appealed for peace between the peoples of Britain and Ireland. "If it were with my latest breath," he urged, "I would entreat you to let the dead bury the dead, and to cast behind you every recollection of bygone evils, to cherish and love and sustain one another throughout all the vicissitudes of human affairs in the times that are to come." Gladstone was tireless in guiding the Bill on its way through the House of Commons; he kept parliament sitting throughout the summer. He won respect even from his enemies. His most formidable opponent was Joseph Chamberlain, and at times excitement was great. Once when Chamberlain was speaking, the Irish members raised the cry of "Judas!" and in the uproar among members on the floor of the House blows were struck. The Queen, when she heard of it, was indignant, and the incident was long remembered as a disgraceful one. The Bill passed in the House of Commons in September by 307 votes to 267.

But the House of Lords rejected the Bill by 419 votes to 41. The Duke of Devonshire (formerly Lord Hartington who had broken with Gladstone in 1886) proposed the rejection, and Lord Salisbury denounced the Bill in the strongest terms:

> If you allow this atrocious, this mean, this treacherous revolution to pass, you will be untrue to the duty which has descended to you from a splendid ancestry; you will be untrue to your highest traditions; you will be untrue to the trust that has been bequeathed to you from the past; you will be untrue to the Empire of England.

The action of the House of Lords brought the struggle, for the time being, to an end. Gladstone himself would have fought on; he wished to dissolve parliament and carry the issue to the country. But the country was not interested in home rule—there was no popular excitement over the defeat of the Bill—and Gladstone's colleagues would not agree to dissolve parliament. Other disagreements with his colleagues followed, and in 1894 he resigned, dying four years later. Lord Rosebery followed Gladstone and was Prime Minister of a Liberal Government until 1895. It was not until 1912 that the government of Asquith introduced the third Home Rule Bill.

3

Imperialism

SINCE WATERLOO THE British people had been largely occupied with their own affairs. Living on an island and with the protection of an all-powerful navy, the British people knew a security unknown to the Continent; they could afford to be insular, they could with impunity feel themselves superior; they could devote themselves to the vast development of industry and trade which made Britain the richest and most powerful country in the world. But three things made contact with foreign nations unavoidable. There was overseas trade; there was emigration—British people went overseas to settle or to trade, and so, almost without knowing it, built up an empire; and there was the need for the government to protect such overseas interests if they should be threatened. On the whole, however, the people were little interested in colonies. The Liberal Party opposed overseas adventures; it stood for free trade, and for the expansion of trade by peaceful means to all parts of the world, not only or chiefly with the colonies. People believed (not unnaturally after the loss of the American colonies in 1783) that colonies would ultimately break away from the mother country, and hence were not of great importance. Even Conservatives could share this view. But by about 1870 a new interest in the Empire began to appear, and Disraeli made use of this interest to give to the Conservative Party a characteristic and distinctive Empire policy.

Disraeli and Imperialism

If the name of Gladstone is for ever associated with the growth of democracy and the struggle for Irish home rule, the name of Disraeli is as closely associated with imperialism. The life of a great nation is many-sided; many different activities are always going on at the same time and many interests are stimulating men to action. It was Disraeli himself who did much to awaken an interest in imperialism; it was he who made monarchy and empire inseparable principles of the Conservative Party. With his Jewish background, his Oriental cast of mind, his lively imagination and originality of thought, he was a man very different from the other great figures of Victorian times. He had travelled widely abroad. Not only, like so many young men of wealth and fashion, had he made the tour of the Rhine and of Italy, but in 1830–1 he had visited the Near East. He had seen the British garrisons in Gibraltar and Malta, he had made expeditions into Spain, he had crossed many territories of the far-flung Turkish Empire, visiting Albania, Athens, Constantinople, Cyprus, Jerusalem and Cairo. He had fallen in love with the calm and the slow-moving life of the Orient. In a letter home he wrote: "I confess that my Turkish prejudices are very much confirmed by my residence in Turkey. The life of the people greatly accords with my taste. . . . To repose on voluptuous ottomans and smoke superb pipes. . . ." These early impressions influenced him later when he took a pro-Turk line against Russia, and helped him to see and notice British interests in the Mediterranean and the Near East, on the great Empire route to India and the East.

Disraeli's imperialism was the result of his imaginative conception of the greatness of India and of the possibilities inherent in the other great territories scattered throughout the world which had come to constitute the British Empire. He could see the possibilities of unification and of the strength which consolidation would bring, and he could see that in this way the British Empire could stand firm throughout the world against any rivals, Russian or German.

Disraeli realised the importance of world affairs, and of

the place of the Empire. In an important speech at Manchester in 1872 he declared:

> I know the difficulty of addressing a body of Englishmen on these topics. The very phrase "foreign affairs" makes an Englishman convinced that I am about to treat of subjects with which he has no concern. Unhappily the relations of England with the rest of the world, which are "foreign affairs", are the matters which most influence his lot. Upon them depends the increase or reduction of taxation. Upon them depends the enjoyment or the embarrassment of his industry.

He went on to refer to changes in the distribution of power in Europe and to the need for a policy of reserve with respect to Europe, but he reminded his audience that the Queen was the sovereign of the most powerful of oriental states, and that "on the other side of the globe there are new establishments belonging to her, teeming with wealth and population, which will, in due time, exercise their influence over the distribution of power". And he appealed to the spirit of the British people "never prouder of the Imperial country to which they belong".

At the Crystal Palace, in the same year, he contrasted the Liberal and Conservative attitudes to the Empire. He accused the Liberals of having followed a policy of disintegrating the Empire:

> It has been proved to all of us that we have lost money by our Colonies. It has been shown with precise, with mathematical demonstration, that there never was a jewel in the Crown of England that was so truly costly as the possession of India. How often has it been suggested that we should at once emancipate ourselves from this incubus!

Granting self-government to the Colonies, he argued, had all but achieved this end. But it was not self-government itself which was at fault. Self-government, however,

> when it was conceded, ought to have been conceded as part of a great policy of Imperial consolidation. It ought to have been accompanied by an Imperial tariff, by securities for the people of England for the enjoyment of the unappropriated

lands which belonged to the Sovereign as their trustee, and by a military code which should have precisely defined the means and the responsibilities by which the Colonies should be defended, and by which, if necessary, this country should call for aid from the Colonies themselves. It ought, further, to have been accompanied by the institution of some representative council in the metropolis, which would have brought the Colonies into constant and continuous relations with the Home Government.

All this, he affirmed, had been omitted because the Colonies had been thought of only in a financial aspect, "totally passing by those moral and political considerations which make nations great, and by the influence of which alone men are distinguished from animals". But the Empire had not disintegrated, he maintained, because of the sympathy of the Colonies for the Mother Country. He called for a new attitude to the Empire, "responding to those distant sympathies which may become the source of incalculable strength and happiness to this land."

This issue is not a mean one. It is whether you will be content to be a comfortable England . . . or whether you will be a great country, an Imperial country, a country where your sons, when they rise, rise to paramount positions, and obtain not merely the esteem of their countrymen, but command the respect of the world.

The Suez Canal and The Queen as Empress of India

When he became Prime Minister, Disraeli brought off two dramatic strokes of imperial policy, the first in 1875 and the second in 1876, both of which strengthened Britain's position in the East. The first bold stroke was to buy on behalf of the British government the Khedive Ismail's shares in the Suez Canal Company, a mainly French concern, which had constructed the canal and opened it to shipping in 1869. The canal had provided a new route to India instead of the long voyage round the Cape of Good Hope. The Khedive (the ruler of Egypt, though strictly viceroy, for Egypt was nominally part of the Turkish Empire) was a spendthrift. To pay his debts he needed to sell his stock (nearly half the total) in the Company. When he was informed of this, Disraeli was quick to see and take the opportunity. The purchase of the stock proved a good investment, it helped to reduce tolls on shipping, largely British, using the canal, and it gave some control over the imperial route. It gave, too, a new interest in Egypt which eventually led to Britain intervening and taking control of the country.

The second of Disraeli's imperial strokes was the Royal Titles Act of 1876. The Prince of Wales undertook a tour in India during the winter of 1875–6. Never before had there been such a visit, and it was an outstanding success. Disraeli felt the time was ripe for a new tie between England and India. By giving the Queen the title of Empress of India the Prime Minister furthered at one and the same time two of his especial interests; he glorified the British monarchy and he enhanced the importance of the Indian Empire. He felt and wanted to make the most of the glamour of monarchy.

Disraeli and the Menace of Russia

Meanwhile, with his special interest in India and the new British route to it, Disraeli saw the great and growing power of Russia as a menace to the British Empire. Throughout the long history of India there had been repeated invasions over the mountains in the north, and now between India and Russia there was only the weak country of Afghanistan. At the same time Russia offered a threat, and indeed a more immediate one, in south-eastern Europe where she was putting herself forward as champion of the Christian peoples of the Balkans who were subjects of the Turkish Empire (which at this time still included most of the Balkan peninsula). There was in Russia a Pan-Slav movement, a movement for bringing together the Slav peoples under Russian leadership, and Russia could well pursue imperialist aims under the guise of protecting Christian peoples from their Turkish, Mohammedan rulers, whose government was ineffective, oppressive and barbarous. If Russia moved south and defeated Turkey, she might secure her ancient dream of Constantinople and a way out into the Mediterranean. Russian warships might then threaten Britain's control of the approaches to the Suez

Canal. In short, British imperialism was confronted by Russian imperialism.

The position was complicated by other factors. Austria-Hungary was also interested in expanding her territories at the expense of the declining Turkish Empire, and Russia, Austria and Germany were working together, linked as they were by the *Dreikaiserbund,* to control the chaotic situation developing in European Turkey. In 1875 the Serbs of Herzegovina rose in revolt against Turkish taxes, and the *Dreikaiserbund* Powers tried to localise the revolt and impose a scheme of reform on the Sultan of Turkey. In the next year Serbia declared war (in support of her brother Serbs under Turkish yoke in Herzegovina), and in Turkey itself a new and stronger sultan, Abdul Hamid, came to power. But meanwhile a most dangerous situation had developed in Turkey's Bulgarian territory. Risings had taken place early in May, and the Turkish government sent in the Bashi-Bazouks, irregular troops, who punished the inhabitants with terrible massacres—12,000 Christians perished in one district alone. Exact official information was slow in coming out, and at first Disraeli tried to minimise the horrors as "to a large extent inventions". But unfortunately the accounts were only too true. The Turkish atrocities gave Gladstone his opportunity. With his pamphlet *The Bulgarian Horrors and the Question of the East,* Gladstone launched a campaign against Disraeli and his policy. He demanded that the Turks should clear out "bag and baggage" from the desolated Bulgaria.

The country was divided. The Queen and the fashionable world supported Disraeli. He discounted the Turkish atrocities, and believed in putting British interests first. He thought it necessary to support Turkey in the face of Russian pressure, even to the point of war. Gladstone, on the other hand, with the Nonconformist conscience behind him, stressed the moral issue: that the Powers of Europe (the Concert of Europe), Christian nations as they were, should help and protect the Christian minorities in the Turkish Empire. He showed a warm ardour for all that seemed to him noble and good. He was prepared even to support Russia in driving the Turks out of Bulgaria. But Gladstone's insight was at its best in seeing that there was not merely a choice between Turkey and Russia. There was a third possibility: national self-government for the peoples of the Balkans.

At last, in April 1877, Russia acted alone. She declared war on Turkey, and her troops moved southward. They were checked, however, in the late summer and winter, and the brave Turkish resistance caused a revulsion of feeling in England. But the weight of Russian numbers was relentless, and by the end of January 1878 the Turks had begged and obtained an armistice. Constantinople was in danger. Already, before the armistice, Britain had taken warning action against Russia: the Mediterranean fleet was ordered through the Dardanelles to Constantinople and parliament was asked to vote a suitable sum for military purposes. The crisis lasted some weeks—there were resignations from the British Cabinet, but war fever flared up among the people. A famous music-hall song added the word "Jingo" to the English language:

We don't want to fight, But by Jingo if we do,
We've got the ships, we've got the men, we've got the money too.

Gladstone's windows in Harley Street were broken by a mob (among the hostile crowd were Parnell and his sister).

The Treaty of San Stefano, signed on March 3rd, 1878, between Turkey and Russia was strongly to Russia's advantage, and was quite unacceptable to the other Powers. Britain called up the reserves, and brought Indian troops to Malta. Russia, however, did not want another, even greater, war and finally agreed to the holding of a European conference. The result was the Congress of Berlin which met in June and July 1878—the most imposing European conference since the Congress of Vienna. Disraeli himself led the British representatives; with him was the Foreign Secretary, Lord Salisbury, who brought with him as secretary his nephew, A. J. Balfour, each destined to be Prime Minister in the future.

The result of the Berlin Congress was that Russia was checked, at least temporarily; she did not gain Constantinople. The big Bulgaria, created by Russia in the San Stefano Treaty, stretching southwards to the Aegean Sea was greatly reduced in size leaving Turkish territory unbroken from the Adriatic to the Black Sea—though this meant Christian Macedonians given up as before to the tender mercy of the Turks and years of misrule and disorder. Britain gained Cyprus, a Mediterranean base from which she could support Turkey. Disraeli and Lord Salisbury returned from Berlin bringing, so they claimed, "Peace with honour." The diplomatic triumph marked the apex of Disraeli's career. The brilliant Jew had risen to be a dominant international figure. "Der alte Jude, das ist der Mann," said Bismarck. And although the settlement of the vexed and persistent Eastern Question was not permanent, there was no war between the Great Powers until 1914.

Difficulties and Abuses of Imperialism

But brilliant as Disraeli's success had appeared in 1878 his policy of imperialism was not one simple succession of triumphs. Imperialism was marked by aggression and war as well as by idealism. British forces—as a result of the fear of Russian intentions in Afghanistan—were sent into that country in 1878, and imposed a settlement. But the British minister and his escort, admitted to the capital, Kabul, were massacred in September 1879. Another campaign followed, and a British force marched to Kabul, though Afghanistan in the end retained its independence (later again, Russian encroachments on the Afghan frontier in 1885 forced Gladstone himself to use the threat of military preparations). In South Africa also Britain became involved in military action. Relations between the Boer settlers in the Transvaal and the native tribes were very bad. Britain feared that the Boers, who were bankrupt, would be overrun by the Zulus, a bold and powerful warrior people, and that the peace of all South Africa might be upset. To prepare for the danger, Britain annexed the Transvaal, making a promise of self-government for the Boers. When war with the Zulus came in 1879, they inflicted a serious defeat on the British at Isandhlwana (January 1879)—the British camp was destroyed and almost all its defenders slain—before they were forced to submit. Such wars were costly in lives and money, and helped to lead to the decline of the government. Gladstone who believed the Afghan or African had his rights as well as the Bulgarian Christian denounced Disraeli's policy most fiercely in his famous Midlothian Campaign. It must be said, however, that the men on the spot in both India and South Africa acted without full authority from the government at home. Distance and slowness of communication made it difficult to control a complicated situation. Disraeli and his ministers at home were not actually pushing a ruthless imperialist policy regardless of all morality and caution. But Disraeli was defeated in the election of 1880, and he died in the following year.

Gladstone was a man of peace, but it was not easy to extricate himself from the difficulties involved in Disraeli's commitments overseas. From Afghanistan British troops were withdrawn successfully. But in South Africa the Boers revolted because self-government seemed slow in coming, and they overwhelmed the British force at Majuba Hill (Natal) in 1881. Nevertheless Gladstone followed out his policy of peace; in spite of loss of prestige, British forces were withdrawn and self-government granted.

Elsewhere, even Gladstone was forced to order military action. In 1882 he sent an army into Egypt in order to put down an anti-European nationalist rising and to restore order. He would have liked this action to have been a matter for the Concert of Europe, but Bismarck was indifferent and France unwilling to act. So Britain acted alone—though John Bright resigned from the Cabinet because he thought the action "a manifest violation of international and moral law". The British intervention was brilliantly successful (because carried out without danger of foreign interference. How unlike Suez in 1956!). The canal was safeguarded, financial interests were protected (British and French investors had lent money to the Khedive), and Britain secured a controlling hand in Egypt. Evelyn Baring, later Lord Cromer, was made Consul-General, and "advised" the Khedive from 1884 to 1907, and during that period Egypt knew a time of orderly government: taxes were lowered, revenues increased, education advanced, irrigation developed and extended, and justice and more effective policing established.

But one thing led to another; intervention in Egypt led to involvement in the Sudan. This territory stretching southwards along the Nile was under Egyptian rule, but its southern portion was in revolt under a fanatical Mohammedan, previously a slave-trader and later an Egyptian official, who had declared himself Mahdi (messiah). It was the British intention to withdraw the Egyptian garrisons from the Sudan, and General Gordon was sent to organise the withdrawal operations. But Gordon formed his own plan: to hold on. He remained in Khartoum, and was cut off by the Mahdi's forces. A long-delayed relief expedition was too late: in January 1885, Khartoum was overwhelmed and Gordon killed. At home the Queen and the public blamed Gladstone for the delay, and a popular mood of anger and hysteria lasted nearly three weeks. But, all the same, the policy of withdrawal from the Sudan was carried out.

Ten years passed. In 1896 the Prime Minister, Lord Salisbury, decided that the time had come to reconquer the Sudan. There were three reasons: to rescue the Sudan from the misrule under which it suffered, to relieve the pressure on the Italians whose army had been destroyed at Adowa by the Abyssinians in the same year, and to maintain British claims to the southern Sudan territories in face of the French, for Salisbury knew that an expedition had been despatched from the French Congo to cross central Africa to the Nile valley. The Anglo-Egyptian forces under Kitchener advanced slowly, building a railway along the Nile. The climax of the campaign was reached at Omdurman in 1898, when the Dervish warriors, now under the Mahdi's son, were mowed down in thousands by field guns and maxims. Khartoum was taken, Gordon avenged, and the Sudan brought under Anglo-Egyptian rule. Almost immediately, with secret instructions from Lord Salisbury, Kitchener moved southwards. At Fashoda he met Marchand and his French party. Kitchener was courteous but firm: he hoisted the British and Egyptian flags. At home the crisis lasted some months: England and France were on the brink of war. Eventually France gave way, Marchand left Fashoda, and early in 1899 England and France agreed to a line dividing their respective interests in the area.

Expansion of British Rule: Africa

Throughout the 1880s and the 1890s British rule was expanding in Burma, Borneo, Malaya, the islands of the Pacific, and above all in Africa. The "Dark Continent" was opened up. Central Africa had been explored by the missionary, David Livingstone, who died there in 1873; he had crossed and recrossed the continent, traced the course of the Zambesi, and discovered Lake Nyasa. In the following years there was a "scramble for Africa": Britain, France, Portugal and Spain had territories there already; now Germans, Italians and Belgians joined in the scramble, and governments backed them and began to compete for African territory. British colonial development went on at first through private enterprise. Bodies of traders, working as chartered companies, followed up their trade by administering the areas where they traded. Statesmanship was slow to realise the opportunities, but Britain—helped by her navy and mercantile marine together with her large financial resources—secured in the end the lion's share. On the western side of Africa Britain gained the hinterland of her older coastal colonies of the Gold Coast, Sierra Leone and Gambia, and also Nigeria; on the eastern side Britain acquired Somaliland, Kenya, Uganda and Nyasaland.

The opening-up of Africa took place without war between the European Powers. Conferences were held, and peaceful agreement was reached as to the division of territories and their boundaries. In particular, Bismarck and Lord Salisbury used their influence to bring about peaceful settlement. In 1884 Bismarck presided over an international conference in Berlin, which gave recognition to the Congo Free State, which later became the Belgian Congo. In 1890 Lord Salisbury achieved notable success with three colonial agreements, with Germany, with France, and with Portugal. The agreement with France was of limited scope, but the settlements with Germany and Portugal were important and, as far as these countries were concerned, virtually completed the partition of Africa.

Meanwhile Cecil Rhodes (1853–1902) was busy expand-

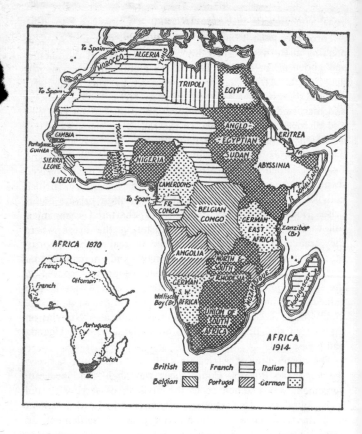

ing British power in South Africa. Rhodes was a country parson's son, who went to South Africa for his health. He made a fortune in the diamond mines, and with wealth came power and influence. Full of the imperial idea, he dreamed of bringing Boers and British into a free partnership and of an all-British railway from Cairo to the Cape. He founded in 1889 the British South Africa Company, which occupied large areas north and west of the Transvaal, areas which became Rhodesia. In 1890 he became Prime Minister of Cape Colony. But five years later he was involved in a plot against

Kruger, the president of the Transvaal, who stood for Boer independence. Dr Jameson (Rhodes' administrator in Rhodesia) led a raid into the Transvaal to aid an expected rising of the Uitlanders, the foreigners working in the Boer state. But the rising did not take place; Jameson was captured, handed over to the British authorities, and imprisoned. Though Rhodes had to resign, his will, when he died in 1902, showed how much he believed in the future of the Anglo-Saxon race: he left a large sum to establish the Rhodes scholarships which bring to Oxford students from the British Dominions, from America, and also some from Germany.

Emigration

Both the Empire and the imperial idea were growing. Emigration provided a safety-valve for increasing population at home; people sought a new life overseas either when poverty pressed or when they were tempted to seek fortune abroad. In the century after 1815 large numbers of people left the British Isles; between ten and fifteen million British people settled overseas during this period. The majority of emigrants, it is true, went to the United States, but there was a steady though lesser stream to Canada and other British territories. In 1880, to take one year as an example, about 166,000 British people emigrated to the United States, and nearly 21,000 to Canada. Those entering Canada were made up of 13,541 English, 3,221 Scots, and 4,140 Irish. This great and prolonged movement of people went on without over-all plan or state organisation, although various societies and individuals did help emigrants to pay their fares. It was often a painful business, such an uprooting of families, but it led to the widening and peopling of the Empire. Canada, for example, steadily developed after the Confederation in 1867; as new territories joined, it came to stretch continuously from Atlantic to Pacific. The completion of the Canadian Pacific Railway in 1885 provided a link between the provinces and assisted immigration.

Imperial Sentiment

Imperial sentiment was voiced by writers and poets, as well as by statesmen. Sir John Seeley, a professor of history at Cambridge, who wrote his *Expansion of England* in 1883, argued that in the future the big states would be dominant. Rudyard Kipling, through his stories and poems, became the popular spokesman of imperialism. Courage, the soldiers' life in camp and foreign field, patriotism—all these had their romantic side. People could easily be carried away by victories and the acquisition of new territories and new wealth. But Kipling also stressed the hard tasks of administration, the "white man's burden". The British must:

> Take up the White Man's burden—
> The savage wars of peace—
> Fill full the mouth of Famine
> And bid the sickness cease.

To Kipling (as he showed in a poem of 1897, the *Recessional*) imperialism was not only pride of Empire, jingoism and racial superiority, but the bringing of civilisation; it was a mission, a responsibility before God:

> God of our fathers, known of old,
> Lord of our far flung battle-line,
> Beneath whose awful Hand we hold
> Dominion over palm and pine—
> Lord God of Hosts, be with us yet,
> Lest we forget—lest we forget!

There was, in fact, genuine idealism behind the idea of Empire. The Empire had been built up almost by accident, and the British had learnt something from the loss of the American colonies. Lord Elton has said that it was the faith and idealism of Wilberforce and Burke that "ensured that the second British Empire would endure because they had ensured that it would be an Empire of an entirely different kind from the first". All the same, selfishness and economic exploitation had its part and Britain built up for herself much trouble for the succeeding century. K. M. Panniker, in the most authoritative Asian study of Western imperialism, insists that the greatest bitterness was caused not by English commercial exploitation but through "the racial superiority". "It is this consciousness of inherent superiority of the European which has won us India," declared Lord Kitchener. "However well educated or clever a native may be, and however brave he may have proved himself, I believe no rank we bestow on him can cause him to be considered the equal of a British officer." This feeling of effortless superiority was to cause untold bitterness and to open the way for Communist exploitation of nationalism in the twentieth century.

Lord Salisbury and Imperialism

Perhaps Lord Salisbury, through his work and character, came to express best of all the genius of imperialism. Soon after he followed Gladstone as Prime Minister in 1886, Salisbury mastered the essentials of the African problems and was free to deal with them in his own way—by firm and patient negotiation. By that time, his biographer [1] has pointed out,

> public opinion was showing pretty clearly that it preferred the idea of Disraeli, J. R. Seeley and J. A. Froude to those of the Liberal Little Englanders. Disraeli's first burst of imperialism had indeed proved too impulsive for the British people and they had turned him out after the Afghan and Zulu wars. Then Gladstone's caution and withdrawals were too much for them in the opposite sense, and they dropped him after his tragic failure in the Sudan. Lord Salisbury now came forward as the reluctant imperialist, and the mood exactly suited public taste.

When Salisbury formed his third government in 1895 he came to occupy a position of unrivalled authority in Britain and abroad. Bismarck had been dismissed by the German Emperor, and Salisbury was regarded as the premier statesman of Europe. His outstanding position clothed with prestige and dignity the power of the Empire over which he presided.

[1] A. L. Kennedy: *Salisbury*, p. 205.

Lord Salisbury was motivated by a desire to do away with slavery by the extension of British influence in Africa and at the same time to bring to that continent "a great civilizing, Christianizing force". Thus the British in their colonies were to act as guardians under whom the black peoples could develop their own distinctive civilization. But he distinguished clearly between the French policy of active intervention by military expeditions and the British method of commercial penetration. In a despatch to the British ambassador in Paris, he wrote,

> The colonial policy of Great Britain and France in West Africa has been widely different. France has overcome by arms . . . Great Britain, on the other hand, has adopted the policy of advance by commercial enterprise. She has not attempted to compete with the military operations of her neighbour.

He pointed out how the British traders of the Niger Company had "without the expenditure of imperial funds, or the sacrifice of the life of a single British soldier, placed under the protection of the Crown the whole of the Lower, and a great portion of the Central, Niger". He emphasised also the importance of free trade—where colonial territories existed they should not give exclusive commercial privileges but should be open to the trade of other nations also.

The solemn character of imperialism was given dramatic form at Queen Victoria's Golden Jubilee of 1887 and Diamond Jubilee of 1897. From all over the Empire princes and prime ministers were invited and came to London. Contingents of Empire troops, in colourful uniforms, marched through the streets of the capital.

Joseph Chamberlain and Imperialism

The growth of Empire had its problems. To some people it appeared that something more definite was needed to strengthen the loose links and hold the Empire together. The idea of imperial federation was suggested; the Empire should have a federal chamber to serve as a central governing body. Joseph Chamberlain, who had left the Liberal Party over home rule for Ireland, favoured a federal development. In 1895 he became Colonial Secretary in Lord Salisbury's government, and from then on he was of all British statesmen the chief exponent of imperialism.

In a speech in the following year, Chamberlain put forward some of his ideas:

> We may endeavour to establish common interests and common obligations. . . . What is the greatest of our common obliga-tions? It is Imperial defence. What is the greatest of our common interests? It is Imperial trade. And those two are very closely connected. . . .

He went on to advocate a "Zollverein for the Empire", that is, free trade within the Empire, with protective duties against foreign countries. And then he concluded with a great dream:

> To organise an Empire—one may almost say to create an Empire—greater and more potent for peace and the civilisation of the world than any that history has yet known—that is a dream if you like, but a dream of which no man need be ashamed.

Chamberlain presided in 1897 over a conference of the prime ministers of the colonies who had come to London for the Jubilee. He put before them suggestions for imperial feder-ation, stressing the need of unity for defence purposes. But only the New Zealand and Tasmanian premiers gave support to this federal idea. The others were not inclined to make formal engagement, and thought the existing loose relationship with Britain was sufficient. The Prime Minister of Canada, Sir Wil-frid Laurier, was justly proud of Canada's position and na-tional identity: he did not think of Canada as "Daughter in my mother's house and mistress in my own", as Kipling had put it, but preferred the loose partnership of sister nations. And indeed it was in this way that the Empire did develop— a partnership without formal ties, tested, since Laurier's time, in two world wars.

Chamberlain's work had more positive effect in the help he gave to the tropical colonies. Where private enterprise was not forthcoming, he made use of public funds to build railways and harbours in Africa; he supported, too, the setting up in England of centres for the study of tropical medicine and botany to improve health and crops. The West Indies were encouraged by grants to their shipping lines and help in marketing their sugar. Cyprus also was helped, by an increased grant. Chamberlain, too, was humanitarian: he used his power against slavery, flogging and the liquor traffic in tropical colonies.

The Boer War

British imperialism suffered disaster with the Boer War (1899–1902). It was the outcome of friction between Boers and British which had been going on for a long time, certainly since 1836 when the Boer farmers had left Cape Colony and trekked northwards to form their new republics of the Transvaal and the Orange Free State. Now, towards the end of the century, there had developed a basic antagonism between two ways of life. The Boers had their old-fashioned, agricultural society, and they saw it threatened by the alien way of life of the Uitlanders (or outsiders), the British and other foreign settlers who had moved in when gold was discovered on the Rand in 1886. The newcomers wanted the vote and rights of citizenship, but the Boers made them wait. But though the Uitlanders had to wait a long term of years for citizenship, they provided through the taxes most of the revenue. In 1898 the Uitlanders found their grievances unbearable, and sent a petition for redress to the Queen.

Thereupon conferences between British and Boer leaders took place, including in 1899, direct conference between the British high commissioner, Milner, and Kruger. But Kruger was an obstinate old man, and the conference failed. The old man could not last for ever, and had Britain waited compromise might in the end have been reached. A young Boer ready to accept compromise was J. C. Smuts, afterwards a good friend of Britain. Neither side, however, was ready to wait indefinitely: public opinion in England was imperialistic, and the Boers were also aggressive. War followed.

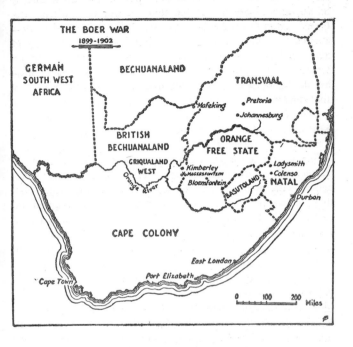

At first the Boers were successful. They knew their country, they were rough farmers accustomed to an open-air life, and they were excellent riders and first-rate marksmen. They invaded Cape Colony and Natal, and laid seige to the towns of Mafeking (defended by Baden-Powell, later founder of the Boy Scouts), Kimberley and Ladysmith. The British troops which were sent northwards to relieve these towns were defeated. "Black Week" was marked by three defeats. But during 1900 large reinforcements were sent out from Britain, and volunteer contingents came from Canada, Australia and New Zealand. With these considerable forces the British were at length able to relieve the besieged towns, and were also able to occupy the Boer capitals of Pretoria and Bloemfontein. The war, by September, appeared to be over. Yet the Boers managed to fight on for nearly two years more, organising themselves into small mobile commandos which carried on an active guerrilla conflict, supplied and assisted from the farms scattered over the veldt. Kitchener, now commander-in-chief, resorted to a policy of rounding up the Boers and their families into special camps. This was to prove a tragic business, as the management of the camps was badly mis-handled. Disease broke out, and mortality among Boer women and children was heavy. Denouncing the camps, the Liberal leader, Campbell-Bannerman, spoke of "methods of bar-barism". At last the Boers sued for peace. In May 1902, peace was made at Vereeniging.

The British terms were generous—and for this Kitchener's statesmanship was largely responsible. The Boer farmers were helped with money grants to set up their farms again, and they were promised self-government. This was granted in 1907, and in 1910 the Union of South Africa (Cape Colony, Natal, the Transvaal and the Orange Free State) was brought into being. But the memory of the war still rankled with the Boers; in fact, it was never forgotten. To British people the war had shown our isolation, that we had no friends in Europe; at home some of the Liberals, notably Lloyd George, opposed the war and sympathised with the Boers. The war of course raised combatant and imperialistic feelings, and there was a mild outburst of street rejoicing at the news of the relief of Mafeking. Looking back today, how-ever, it may seem that the Boer War brought to an end the confident period of British imperialism.

4

Wealth, Poverty and the Beginnings of Socialism

Britain and Industrial Growth

BY 1868 INDUSTRY was becoming the dominant characteristic of north-western Europe. The industrial revolution in England was followed by a continuous process of development, never stopping, spreading to our neighbours in western Europe, and ultimately making itself felt in the most distant countries. Change, progress, were going on in every direction: the age of steel followed the age of iron. The Bessemer process (1856), the method of Siemens, and the Gilchrist Thomas process (1878), all ways of making cheap steel, enabled steel to take the place of the weaker iron. Steel rails came to replace iron rails, and gave their railway track a longer life; steel hulls and better engines were made for ships. British steel production increased over twenty-two times between 1870 and 1900; German and American production also greatly expanded, American output being twice the British by the end of the century. Britain and Europe were being more and more closely linked with distant lands, and natural objects were being overcome: the cable to America was laid in 1866, the Suez Canal was opened in 1869, the trans-continental railway link-up in America took place in the same year, the driving of the Mont Cenis tunnel through the Alps was completed in 1871, and in the next year work on the St Gotthard commenced, Bell demonstrated his telephone in 1876. South and eastern Europe, especially the Balkans and Russia, remained, in contrast, primitive and undeveloped—peasant life went on much as it had in the Middle Ages. The peasants of, for example, Serbia or Albania, were now left far behind by the industrial workers of the west. Industry—machine production motivated by steam—brought power, a rising standard of life, and a way of life unknown before.

As early as 1830 the English writer of an economic tract had pointed out very clearly the advantages of machinery. He asked his countrymen "to reflect on the means which have raised mankind to their actual state of knowledge, of civilisation, and of comparative comforts; and he is confident of their being convinced that the whole progress is entirely owing to the invention of contrivances for facilitating labour and rendering it more productive". The pamphlet showed briefly how man's growing control over nature had conditioned human development: first men were hunters, then the spade and pick gave limited power over the soil, next the plough, and the loom, and more recently command over coal and minerals, and the steam engine. And thus—pointing the economic moral of the industrial age—machinery introduced for private profit had brought about public good.

Britain, in 1870, was still in the van of economic progress, still unrivalled as an industrial nation, the greatest, in fact, in the world. At that time Britain had a greater mileage of railways than Germany or France (the European countries nearest to her in industrial growth), and produced far more coal, iron and steel than either of those countries. Britain's volume of external trade (i.e., the total of goods coming into, and going out of, the country) was greater than that of Germany, France and Italy put together, and was between three and four times greater than that of the U.S.A.

Great, however, as were Britain's advantages as an industrial nation, some of these advantages were simply due to her having gone through the industrial revolution before other nations. These nations would, in time, catch up. And Britain was coming to depend not simply upon using her own resources and manufactured goods for her own needs, but on using her manufactured goods to purchase food and raw materials from abroad. As an economic writer [1] stated in 1868,

England's position is not that of a great landed proprietor, with an assured revenue. . . . It is that of a great merchant, who by immense skill and capital has gained the front rank, and developed an enormous commerce, but has to support an ever-increasing host of dependents. He has to encounter the risks of trade, and to face jealous rivals, and can only depend on continued good judgment and fortune, and the help of God, to maintain himself and his successors in the foremost place among the nations of the world.

The same writer, referring to the great British increase in wealth, said:

How long this increase will last, and at what rate, is beyond human power to predict. England is more favourably situated than any country, except the United States, for manufactures and commerce; and the demand for these must augment continually with the spread of civilization and railways among the . . . population of the world. The future rise of the United States into a great manufacturing and naval power, appears the most probable and certain cause which will place a limit to our national increase and prosperity.

Once more he sounded a note of warning when he said:

The income of England is the largest of any nation, and shows wonderful good fortune and prosperity; but we must not forget that it rests on an unstable foundation. The turn of trade, or obstinacy and short-sightedness in our working classes, or a great naval war, may drive us from the markets of the world, and bring down our auxiliary as well as our productive industries.

Britain did, in fact, maintain her great and proud place for many years to come. Britain was the workshop of the world. The period 1865–75 was one of rapid economic growth, and much of the wealth produced was reinvested, with an eye to the future. More capital and labour were

1 R. Dudley Baxter: *National Income* (1868).

invested in the textile industry. Here Britain surpassed all other countries. Cotton was particularly important; the demand for cotton goods at home and abroad was very large, and it was increasing. Britain's entry into the age of steel—the metal fundamental to development in industrial machinery, railways and shipping—has been remarked. Along with the increased production of steel went the development of the iron and coal industries—British production of coal almost doubled between 1870 and 1900. With increased quantities of cheap steel came improvements in mechanical engineering, in machine-tools, and in the machinery produced, and also a great increase in the amount of machinery. Machinery came more and more into use, not only in the great industries but in smaller ones also.

Great developments went on in shipping. During the first half of the nineteenth century the screw propeller had replaced the paddle-wheels of the earliest steamboats. Then the steam engines were greatly improved, so reducing fuel consumption and allowing the ships to travel much farther. Parsons invented the steam turbine engine in 1884, and by about 1900 ships were equipped with it. Shipbuilding was itself an important industry—concentrated on the Clyde, on Tyneside and at Birkenhead, and across the Irish Sea at Belfast. There, after 1860, Harland and Wolff (an immigrant from Germany) developed their shipyards which later became the largest in the world. Shipbuilding yards and merchant ships made necessary the building or extension of docks. During the second half of the century there were new docks or extensions in London, Tilbury, Liverpool, the Mersey, Southampton, Barrow-in-Furness, Grimsby, Cardiff and Bristol. All this was part of a great expansion of seaborne trade. Steamships did on the oceans what the railways had done on land—goods could be brought across the water at no greater cost than would have been necessary to move them, in earlier times, a few miles by land. The opening of the Suez Canal provided, too, a shorter route to the East—India, China, Australia and New Zealand—taking the place of the old way around the Cape of Good Hope. China, Japan, Malaya and Siam were all offering new markets to British trade.

New lands were opened up overseas. The prairies of the midwest in America were slowly being settled, and the railways could carry their corn to the ports for shipment to Britain. Her manufactured goods went back in exchange. In South America, new opportunities opened up in the Argentine. British merchants were sending their goods there, setting up offices in Buenos Aires, and investing capital in factories and railways. In 1889 the Argentine began shipping cattle to England; meanwhile, by about 1880, refrigeration was perfected, and by 1900 frozen meat was being imported regularly in immense quantities from the Argentine, Australia and New Zealand. Refrigeration also made possible the import of dairy products and of fruit and vegetables.

The industrial revolution in England and the vast expansion of industry and trade which followed were the work of private enterprise. Small capital and little education were necessary for a man to set up in business. It was an age of competition; hard work, brains and ingenuity would bring their own reward—Samuel Smiles had written his *Self-Help* in 1859. Even the great scientists of the first half of the nineteenth century were, like the business people, self-made men; Davy and Faraday had "picked up" their scientific knowledge, for there was then no broad highway of science courses in schools, universities and technical colleges. As time went on this state of affairs became dangerous. International exhibitions, such as the Great Exhibition of 1851 and the Paris Exhibition of 1867, showed that foreign craftsmen were developing their own skills and coming to rival those of Britain. It was pointed out in 1867 by a British manufacturer who knew Germany that education was giving Germany the advantage over us:

> The education of Germany is the result of a national organisation which compels every peasant to send his children to school, and afterwards affords the opportunity of acquiring such technical knowledge as may be useful in the department of industry to which they are destined. . . . If we continue to fight with our present voluntary system we shall be defeated.

The warning was timely. And in 1870 the Education Act

did provide a system of Board schools for elementary education. In the following years elementary education was made compulsory and free. During these years, too, new university colleges were being founded, and a number of technical colleges as well. Chemistry, physics, geology, and the various branches of engineering developed as distinct bodies of knowledge which had to be studied before anyone could hope to make further scientific or technical progress in the industrial field, and regular courses were worked out for the schools and higher institutions. Industry and industrial research became a matter for the specialist.

Huskisson, Peel and Gladstone had given Britain free trade. During the period of her industrial and commercial supremacy, Britain did not need protection, for her trade was expanding. What suited her best was not the old policy of restriction and protection, but the vast expansion of trade all over the world. The growth of world trade could not be a one-way traffic. If Britain was to export more and more goods, she must be prepared to take foreign goods in return. Free traders believed not only that free exchange would bring prosperity but also that it would make for international peace. For world exchange of goods would make the nations interdependent. War would be folly—to make war on one's customers, disrupt the flow of goods and dislocate the intricate arrangements of credit. This belief contributed to a feeling of security in mid-Victorian England. While British exports of manufactured goods were increasing to pay for the import of the foodstuffs and raw materials she needed, the country was greatly helped also by her so-called "invisible" exports. These were made up of foreign investments, and shipping, insurance and banking services. The payments which foreigners made for these meant that Britain could import goods to a greater value than that of the goods she exported—the difference was covered by the invisible exports.

All this has been well summarised by a modern economic historian:

To save abundantly and invest prudently; to develop foreign markets and to be ready to supply them with the kind of goods they could most plentifully absorb; to concentrate productive resources on the enlargment of capital equipment, on providing the basic necessities of existence while paying little attention to luxuries, and on the development of those business services which the whole trading world required; to improve productive techniques in the main occupations where practicable and, having done so, to specialize on those where the greatest comparative advantage was attained—these were the tasks which the mid-Victorians attempted.

And the same authority points out: "It is the astonishing dynamic quality that is the outstanding economic characteristic of the mid-Victorian period"; and, as for its result: "If the accumulation of wealth and its application to further accumulation is taken as the criterion of economic success then this was a very successful age." [2]

Trade Rivals

Towards the end of the century industrial rivals did begin to surpass Britain. By 1900 the United States was producing more coal than Britain, and both the United States and Germany were producing more steel than Britain. This did not mean that British industry was stationary; in fact, its output doubled between 1870 and 1913. But its rivals were producing even more than Britain: the United States' output of manufactured goods surpassed that of Britain by the 1880s, and German output passed the British early in the next century. Other countries also, such as France, Belgium, Sweden, Russia and Italy, though not as highly industrialised as Britain, made very important advances. In population, too, her great industrial competitors were moving ahead of Britain. In 1870 the population of Germany was 41 millions, of the United States 38 millions, and the United Kingdom 32 millions; in 1900 they were 56, 80 and 41 millions.

All these things were signs of a decline in Britain's relative strength. But between 1870 and 1913 international trade about trebled. With this vast increase Britain could still hold her own, and she was greatly helped by the consequent increase—with the general increase of trade—of her invisible exports. Opportunities for investment abroad were multiplied

2 W. Ashworth: *Economic History of England 1870–1939*, p. 21 and p. 7.

as new lands were opened out, and the expanded volume of world trade brought to Britain a greatly increased demand for her shipping, insurance and banking services. At the turn of the century, too, a new industrial revolution was beginning, with the development of electric power and the internal combustion engine. Both these became important in the next reign. Electricity brought the telegraph, the telephone, electric lighting (developed by Edison in America about 1880), and wireless—Marconi sent the first Morse code wireless signals across the Atlantic in 1901. The German invention of the internal combustion engine—various inventors had been at work since the 1860s—led in the 1890s to the motor car and a little later to the aeroplane (in 1903 the Wright brothers made the first flight in America). These were great advances. And, although Britain was not alone in the field as she had been in the first industrial revolution, she was able to hold her own in the foremost rank of industrial nations.

Poor and Rich

Britain passed through the radical economic and social changes of industrialisation and at the same time established a democratic system of government, without violent revolution. There were nevertheless causes enough for discontent, in the long hours and hard lives of the working people, and in the grinding poverty of the badly paid or those with only casual employment. The families of the poor had a long and severe struggle to get proper education for clever children when the state provided nothing more than elementary schooling. A careful enquiry made by a retired shipowner, Charles Booth, the first volume of whose *Life and Labour of the People of London* was published in 1889, showed that in London thirty per cent. of the population of the world's richest city lived in poverty; their food, clothes and housing were not sufficient to keep them in a decent physical condition. Similar enquiries were later made in other cities, and it was clear that all industrial towns contained many people, chiefly in the unskilled labourer class, who lived in want, ill-health and misery. In the country, too, farm labourers were in a bad way; their pay was about half that of factory hands, and as they could not easily combine in a union to protect themselves, they were more liable to tyrannical treatment by their masters.

To the upper and middle classes Victorian Britain offered a full and agreeable life, for servants were cheap and easily found. The domestic servant or maid did the household work in days before gadgets and labour-saving devices, and when private houses were still large. She carried water in cans or jugs to the bedrooms and lit coal fires in the living-rooms. For the poor, on the other hand, there was little save casual employment, casual charity, the workhouse and the police.

Charity and Self-help

There had, of course, always been private charity. The growth of population and the spread of industrial slums, however, created new and difficult problems with which casual charity could not cope efficiently or completely. But economists taught that it was best not to interfere with private business men in making and spending money, and that the government could not prevent poverty. And so it was left to individuals and voluntary societies to deal with want and suffering. Money and goods were collected privately and distributed to the aged and the sick. Two notable examples of private effort which developed into nation-wide organisations were Dr Barnardo's Homes and the Salvation Army. Dr Barnardo's first home for destitute children was opened in London in 1867, and by 1905 there were 112 district homes. Homeless children were found, fed, clothed, housed and educated. Training for jobs, for the navy and mercantile marine, and an emigration scheme to Canada all played a part. The Salvation Army was created by William Booth (1829–1912), and aimed at improving the spiritual life of the people. It brought religion out of the churches and to the people by popular methods, the street-corner meeting and the brass band. But social needs were not neglected— there were night shelters, homes for the destitute, and also provision for training the unemployed, and big emigration schemes.

Apart from charitable organisations, independent movements also came into existence in which the workers set out to help themselves. Such were the co-operative movement, the trade unions, and the socialist movement, and all these were to grow greatly and become factors of vast and continuing importance in British life. There were also the friendly societies, which had many members, and whose funds contributed to their assistance in hard times.

Trade Unions

The trade unions had been formed by workers, naturally with the immediate intention of advancing the worker's interests, by improving wages, hours and conditions of labour. The individual labourer was often powerless to improve his conditions, but when a number of labourers combined into a union they could bargain with an employer. When the unions grew in size and strength, they were able—once the town artisans had got the vote by the Reform Act of 1867— to exert pressure on the government. They were able to do this in spite of a good deal of criticism, opposition and resistance from the employers and the well-to-do generally, and not surprisingly unions did not always act in the best or wisest way. There were, indeed, some deeds of violence by unionists against non-unionists, to make them join and pay the subscription. Eventually both Gladstone and Disraeli found themselves forced to give attention to the making of laws to regulate and improve the trade union position. Unions were given protection against embezzlement of their funds, just as the property of any other lawful association of people was protected; they were freed from the old common law against conspiracy which had made their legal position difficult and uncertain if they organised a strike, and they were allowed peaceful picketing during strikes.

In 1868 the unions began to meet together in an annual Trades Union Congress. The election of 1874 brought to the House of Commons the first working-class M.Ps, Thomas Burt and Alexander Macdonald, both miners. Macdonald was the son of a Lanarkshire miner, and had himself started to work in the pit when eight years old. As a young man he had saved enough to go to Glasgow University, and became a teacher for a few years. But he devoted most of his life to helping the miners—he was elected president of the National Union of Miners in 1863. The Miners' Conference of that year opened with prayer—an interesting feature which illustrates the religious outlook typical of their leaders, mostly Nonconformists—and under Macdonald's lead they worked out their programme of reform. The miners aimed at a reduction of hours, better conditions of work, an end to the truck system (payment of wages partly in kind), and the right of the men to appoint checkweighers, that is, their own representatives who checked the amount of coal produced, on which each man's pay was based.

Unionism developed more successfully in some industries than in others; it had a very difficult start in agriculture. In the early 1870s Joseph Arch, a Warwickshire farmhand and lay preacher, organised the Agricultural Labourers' Union, but it did not last. About 1875 a decline in agriculture set in due to the importation of American wheat, and there was widespread unemployment among farm labourers. They were only too eager to get jobs on the farmers' conditions, and they had no money to pay their union fees. Their union faded out altogether in 1894. The Amalgamated Society of Railway Servants, formed in 1872, also had a hard struggle for existence. The railway companies argued that a railway must have the same kind of discipline as an army, in order to give safety and efficiency, and the railway companies were very reluctant to recognise the unions.

Among the early trade unionists most were skilled workers —for it was the best trained and most serious men who could see the purpose of a union. The unskilled workers were much more difficult to organise. The first permanent union of this kind was that of the London Dockers, first formed on a very small scale in 1887. Two years later the dockers organised a great strike, and paralysed the London docks for a month, but the men avoided violence and won wide support and financial help which enabled them to draw strike pay. Eventually they won their demands, a rise giving them a standard rate of 6d. an hour, extra pay for overtime, and four hours fixed as a minimum period of engagement. About the same time, successes had been won by other poorly paid workers, including the London match-girls (whose work was making matches) and the gas workers. Great public sympathy was shown for the workers, and employers were criticised. The unions were proving successful, and it was clear also that there was a public conscience. Other people were coming to realise that the workers' lot needed improvement. Nevertheless union membership among the unskilled declined in the 1890s, and did not really recover until about 1910.

The Co-operative Movement

The co-operative movement—of stores or shops run by working-class people for the working classes—was also growing into an important organisation. From humble beginnings with the first shop in Toad Lane, Rochdale, in 1844, the shops or stores had spread through Lancashire and Yorkshire, into Scotland and the Midlands, and lastly to the more conservative London and the southern counties. In 1863 the Co-operative Wholesale Society started in Manchester: this was an organisation formed by the retail co-operative shops to make wholesale purchases on their behalf—the wholesale organisation, since it made bulk purchases, could usually buy more cheaply than a single small shop could. The C.W.S. went along rather slowly for twenty years, but eventually became a very large trading organisation.

Whereas the trade union was a powerful instrument in the workers' hands, it may not be so clear how the co-operative movement served the workers. In fact, the co-operative movement helped them in at least three ways: the retail stores gave good value for money; the profit was shared among members according to the value of their purchases, and this share or dividend could be left to accumulate at interest, so encouraging thrift; and the stores encouraged democracy, for each store was managed by a committee elected by the members of the local co-operative society. In addition, the co-operative movement turned some of its profits to educational ends, such as classes for its members. Business profit and educational advance were allied; hard-headed common sense was not divorced from social idealism.

Socialism

Private charity and co-operation and trade unions were all directed towards limited and definite objects. But there was another workers' movement which had no single limited object. This movement was socialism—it was aimed not at any one reform here or there but at changing the whole social order in the interest of the workers. Socialism was a direct result of the Industrial Revolution, which had created the conditions in which such an idea could flourish. The changes in industry had led to large-scale production and the employment in the factories of large numbers of workers, and had made more general a clear-cut distinction between capitalists, who "owned" an industry, and workers, who merely worked in it. Capitalists and workers looked at things in different ways. The capitalists and economists said: Leave industry to the capitalist, and his self-interest will lead him to produce as much wealth as possible, from which he will grow rich himself, and by using his money, benefit society. The socialists said: Private capitalism means low wages, long hours, slum houses, everything on the cheap to enable the capitalist to make profits. Take industry out of the hands of private owners and business men, and run the industrial system for the common good.

Of course, in good times people did not listen much to the socialist arguments. When industry was expanding and there were plenty of jobs, there was little socialism. But when things went badly, people began to think about socialism. In 1875 the agricultural depression set in. The home market was flooded, and cheap grain began to pour in from the vast, newly developed wheatfields of the United States, fields large enough to make full use of the combine harvester, at that time little used in Britain. The new railways in America and Atlantic steam shipping brought the grain to Britain in great quantities. Much grain also came in sailing vessels—in this trade sail long competed successfully with steam—and some of the grain came from Pacific ports all the way round Cape Horn. The American grain could be sold more cheaply than British grain. British prices dropped. Refrigeration also enabled overseas producers to send meat and butter to be sold in Britain (though sales of home-produced meat increased, and livestock farming suffered little). The depression became even worse in 1891–2. Not only was it depression, but prolonged depression. Farmers were faced with ruin; they dismissed labourers, and so there was unemployment and great distress.

At such times younger men could leave the country and look for work in the towns, or emigrate to countries overseas to take up a life for which a farming stock was particularly well suited. But it was not so easy to find work in the towns at home, for in the 1880s there was depression in industry as well as in agriculture. Britain had had a good period as workshop of the world, because the Industrial Revolution had taken place there first and given a good start. Germany and America, however, were now fast developing their own industries, and beginning to compete with British manufactured goods. Difficulties of this kind did make people realise that industrial expansion and consequent prosperity were not necessarily to go on for ever. Unemployment, more than anything else, was likely to make the workers listen to socialist arguments and think of socialism as a remedy for their distress.

Many years before, when he was a young man, Disraeli in his novel *Sybil; or, The Two Nations* (published in 1845) had contrasted the two nations—the two social classes—which existed in England. On the one hand there was riches and luxury, on the other poverty and misery. He had implied his own "conviction that the rights of labour were as sacred as those of property . . . that the social happiness of the millions should be the first object of a statesman." Disraeli looked to the younger generation of the English aristocracy as "the natural Leaders of the People". Only two years after Disraeli, Karl Marx was writing in the *Communist Manifesto*: "More and more, society is splitting into two great hostile camps, into two great and directly contraposed classes: bourgeoisie and proletariat." But Marx was to look for social salvation to an organised party of the workers themselves.

It was this Karl Marx, a German Jew exiled from Germany

on account of his political activities, who developed the most extreme socialist doctrine. He spent much of his life studying and writing in London, and tried to put forward a scientific theory of socialism. He wrote the *Communist Manifesto* in 1847, and a long, solid work, *Das Kapital,* the first volume of which was published in 1867. Marx developed his idea of the class war: the rich against the poor. He argued that the rich get richer by exploiting the poor, and the poor get poorer. The wealth of the rich would come to be concentrated into fewer and fewer hands; great monopolies would grow up, and small businesses disappear. The workers would be more and more exploited, and their lot would be one of increasing misery. But inevitably with the growth of large-scale production, the factory system would bring them together in large numbers; the workers would unite. At last they would break out in a violent revolution; they would overthrow the capitalists, seize control of the monopolies, and work the industrial system themselves and for themselves. Marx's theory had immense influence on the Continent; it was taken up by Lenin and lay behind the Russian Revolution of 1917.

Marx's theories, however, had little effect in Britain, largely because most of the early trade union leaders, unlike their continental counterparts, drew their inspiration from Christianity. Like the Tolpuddle Martyrs at the beginning of the century, they fought without bitterness for the rights of their fellows. As a result the idea of class war did not interfere with the slow, measured development of British institutions: the steady growth of a democratic system in central and local government, and the gradual improvement of social conditions both by law and as a result of public opinion. Many workers' leaders considered that, as private enterprise was creating great wealth, it was better to work with it rather than against it. Nor did the rich, the capitalists, become fewer. As joint-stock companies with limited liability grew up, a large number of small shareholders invested in industry and became capitalists. And so there were more capitalists as capitalism developed in Britain, not fewer as Marx had supposed.

There was, however, one Marxist society advocating a

working-class revolution to overthrow the governing class. This was the Social Democratic Federation, which began in 1881 as the Democratic Federation. Its founder was H. M. Hyndman, a well-to-do man, who had studied Marx; and William Morris, the artist, craftsman and poet, was a member for a short time. The S.D.F. organised some large meetings and marches of the unemployed during the winter of 1885–6. But the leaders split among themselves, and the disagreements made the movement ineffective. The Fabian Society, founded in 1884, which was less impressed by Marxian ideas, was more influential in this country. Among its members were the dramatist, Bernard Shaw, and the economists, Sidney and Beatrice Webb. The Fabians took their name from the Roman general, Fabius, who had believed in fighting Hannibal by a cautious policy of gradual advances rather than by a pitched battle; they believed that socialism could come about gradually by peaceful and democratic means. To this end, they set about educating public opinion by means of publications called the *Fabian Essays*, by meetings and discussion, and by working in local government and getting their ideas slowly adopted. Bernard Shaw dealt in his plays with many topical social issues; by making people laugh at abuses and follies he awakened their power of criticism and stimulated ideas of social reform.

Many other influences also helped to awaken people to a realisation of social evils and made them think of socialism as a solution. One of these influences was the writer Robert Blatchford. He was an ex-soldier, but he had the gift of vigorous and effective writing. He started a very popular socialist weekly, the *Clarion*, in 1891. Even today one can read his books, *Merrie England* and *Britain for the British*, with enjoyment and interest. He did not hate the rich so much as feel a genuine sympathy for the poor and the underdog. He was an attractive character, and he aroused considerable popular attention.

Working-class candidates were beginning to get into Parliament. The two miners had been elected in 1874; by 1885 there were eleven working-class M.Ps. Most of these mainly sat with the Liberals, and were sometimes referred to by the term "Lib-Lab". But in 1893 a new direction was taken by the working-class movement—towards independence. The Independent Labour Party was founded with Keir Hardie as chairman. Hardie had started work in the coal mines at the age of ten. He was a Scot, of marked integrity, a straightforward man, who became a devoted leader of the workers' cause. He often said that "the Christianity of Christ" was "the chief inspiration and driving force" of his life. When he was elected to the House of Commons in 1892 he appeared in his miner's cap and rough tweed suit, and was conspicuous among the top hats and frock coats which members wore in those days, but eventually he won respect. At first his I.L.P. made no headway, but Hardie came to see that he must gain the support of the trade unions with their big membership and large funds before a Labour Party could become a practical proposition.

In 1900 a meeting was arranged in London between representatives of the I.L.P., the Fabians, the old S.D.F., and the trade unions. At this meeting they all agreed to support a Labour Representation Committee, and in the same year, two of its candidates, of whom Hardie was one, were elected to parliament. In 1906 the L.R.C. became the Labour Party, when twenty-nine of its members were elected to parliament in the General Election of that year. Among them were Ramsay MacDonald and Philip Snowden, who were, eighteen years later, to be Prime Minister and Chancellor of the Exchequer in the first Labour Government ever formed in the United Kingdom. Such were the origins of socialism in this country and the beginnings of the Labour Party, which, though small at first, was destined after the First World War to replace the Liberal Party as the second of the two great parties in the state.

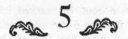

5

Characteristics of the Later Victorian Age

SO FAR THE story in this volume has been one of growth and development, of the overcoming of obstacles and difficulties, and of the mounting strength and greatness of the nation. The extension of democratic government, new freedom and opportunity for the individual, the expansion of the Empire overseas, Britain as the greatest industrial and commercial nation of the world—all these are features of the period between 1868 and the death of the Queen, all testify to certain characteristics of the age, Victorian faith, confidence and optimism, Victorian energy, and—solid, practical and substantial—Victorian achievement. With them go the great reforms of the early Victorian period, such as are associated with the name of Lord Shaftesbury, and a far greater humanity of the upper classes *vis-à-vis* the rulers of eighteenth-century England. All this is true—and yet there is another side to it. For people who were brought up in the shadow of the Victorian age, people whose parents were themselves Victorians, the adjective "Victorian" may have a different, a definite though doubtless ill-defined, significance. The term "Victorian" will recall a sense of being cramped, of strict discipline in the home, of piety in a narrow form, of prudery, perhaps, or even hypocrisy, certainly of ugliness and dullness, associated with heavy furniture, too much decoration, dark clumsy clothing, solemn, pompous public monuments and buildings and cheap, poor, standardised dwellings and city streets.

These conflicting pictures represent or reflect different aspects of the Victorian scene. Above all people had, in Victorian times, a sense of serious purpose in life. They worked hard at the things they thought important and worthwhile because they thought it their duty to do so; they worked hard at the tasks which had been put before them. Scientific and technical development and the new organisation of factory labour in large-scale production had given the opportunity to produce more and more wealth. The Victorian business man and workman worked hard each at his own task, and the result was material success—the multiplication of material goods in quantities never known before. At the same time they looked askance at anything which would hinder the economic process: at any kind of dissipation, drinking, or idleness, even at what appeared a waste of time in unproductive pursuits. In literature, what was useful was most valued—that is to say, what was morally edifying, and what taught the virtues of hard work, thrift and self-denial. Ugly and cheap much of their building was—because railway transport made it possible to carry the cheapest building materials—bricks and slate—all over the country wherever they were required. But it must be remembered to the credit of the Victorians that they solved the problems of city sanitation by building proper sewage systems. Early Victorian housing and public health were unbelievably bad, but the greatest improvements had been made before our period opens—the last severe cholera epidemic was in 1865.

Victorian Religion: Evangelicalism

At the centre of Victorian life was religion. It has been well said by a modern historian, himself a Victorian,

No one will ever understand Victorian England who does not appreciate that among highly civilised, in contradistinction to more primitive, countries it was one of the most religious that the world has known. Moreover its particular type of Christianity laid a particularly direct emphasis upon conduct . . . it was in practice very largely a doctrine of salvation by works.[1]

[1] R. C. K. Ensor: *England, 1870–1914*, p. 137.

This type of religion was known as Evangelicalism, as it was based on the teaching of the Gospels (the Evangels), and stressed in addition to the necessity of faith the need for doing good works and living a Christian life. It was the dominant form of religion at the time, and motivated both churchmen and Nonconformists. In its broadest sense it influenced high churchmen such as Gladstone and Salisbury; it influenced also the scientist and agnostic, T. H. Huxley, who showed a similar fervour and moral sense in his agnosticism; and it can be seen in the imperialism of Kipling with its "white man's burden" and his famous *Recessional* which found its way into the hymn books.

Evangelicalism was marked by certain definite features. There was a stress on the literal truth of the Bible, which gave Christians a strong position so long as the Holy Book was virtually unchallenged but proved a disadvantage when a more flexible position could have been better defended against attacks which were based on valid or partly valid criticism. Then there was among the Evangelicals a firm belief in rewards and punishments to come in an after life. As the historian quoted above put it:

If one asks how nineteenth-century English merchants earned the reputation of being the most honest in the world (a very real factor in the nineteeth-century of primary English trade), the answer is because hell and heaven seemed as certain to them as tomorrow's sunrise, and the Last Judgement as real as the week's balance-sheet. This keen sense of moral accountancy had also much to do with the success of self-government in the political sphere.

And along with the certainty of rewards and punishments to come in the next world went the conviction that this life was simply a preparation for the next: one was in the world to be tried and tested, to work and to grow in moral stature to fit oneself for the life in heaven. It was an all-important matter, therefore, a practical proposition for a businesslike person, to put pleasure aside and to live a life of duty, sobriety and hard work. These features of Evangelicalism gave to Victorian England very great strength.

Of course, the teachings of Christianity were common

ground everywhere in Europe. Anywhere in Europe the particular features which were characteristic of Evangelicalism *might* have become dominant. One might ask: Was it Evangelicalism which produced Victorian England, or was it Victorian England that produced Evangelicalism? Whatever the answer may be, it is certain that the principles of Evangelicalism were such as to confirm and inspire the inherent, dynamic tendencies of an industrial and commercial age. Another modern writer on the Victorians has described Evangelicalism as "the moral cement of English Society", and a third has said: "To be serious, to redeem the time, to abstain from gambling, to remember the Sabbath Day to keep it holy, to limit the gratification of the senses to the pleasures of a table lawfully earned, and the embraces of a wife lawfully wedded, are virtues for which the reward is not laid up in Heaven only." In short, the hard and narrow way of salvation was also the road to prosperity and respectability.

Organised religion took a central part in men's lives and, in an age before the cinema, radio and television, there was a greater interest in church- and chapel-going, in hymn singing, and in sermons, just as there was also in politics and the speeches of political leaders in parliament. Almost everywhere, in country and town, people attended church regularly every Sunday, many people attended two or three services, and children went to Sunday schools. During the week also the chapels held prayer-meetings. Only in the largest cities were there considerable areas where people did not go to church or chapel—such people made a new "heathen", the poorest and most degraded elements which responded but little to the missionary efforts made on their behalf by believers. In private houses, too, family prayers were the rule, certainly among the upper and middle classes. Sunday itself was completely given up to religion, for no games, sports or entertainments were allowed. Even reading was confined to religious works, the Bible itself, or serious books and magazines specially produced for Sunday reading. Thus it was that books of sermons had a large sale; popular preachers drew immense crowds to hear them, and their sermons could later reach a much larger congregation through the printed page. Perhaps the most renowned preacher of all was the Baptist, C. H. Spurgeon (1834–92).

Spurgeon preached that salvation by grace must lead to good living, "that they which have believed in God must be careful to maintain good works". Faith and works would result in good and holy lives, and such lives would bring their own reward, both in the next world and this. In one sermon of 1888 he declared: "Tradesmen who are esteemed for integrity, merchants who bargain to their own hurt but change not, dealers who can be trusted in the market with uncounted gold, your acts are good and profitable both to the church and to the world." And again, in a sermon of 1851, he spoke of the great importance of a God-fearing example both by parents at home in the family and by a church to its members:

I know a little humble Dissenting chapel, of the straitest sect of our religion. Culture there was none in the ministry; but the people were staunch believers . . . learned to believe, and to live upon it. . . . Five or six families came out of that place, and became substantial in wealth, and generous in liberality. These all sprang from plain, humble men, who knew their Bible, and believed the doctrines of grace. They learned to fear God, and to trust in Him, and to rest in the old faith, and even in worldly things they prospered. . . . These men were fed on substantial meat, and they became sturdy old fellows, able to cope with the world, and fight their way. I would to God that we had more men today who would maintain truth at all hazards.

Spurgeon could already see the dangers of a decline in the sturdy spirit of earlier days. He went on to speak of "the gutta-percha backbone" as being common among Nonconformists, and of their taking to politics and "the new philosophy"; all this he feared would lead to a loss of force in their testimony and to a decrease in numbers. He saw, too, the danger that Victorian prosperity by its very success might come to defeat itself. In another sermon of 1891, he said:

Among the dangers to Christian men, the greatest, perhaps, is accumulating wealth—the danger of prosperity. Wesley used

sometimes to fear that Christianity was self-destructive; for
when a man becomes a Christian, the blessings of this life
are his, too: he begins to rise in the world; he leaves his old
position behind him; and, alas! too often, with increasing
riches, forgets the God who gave him all. . . . May God grant
that we may never turn his mercies into an excuse for sinning
against him! You who are rich have no more liberty to sin
than if you were poor. . . . We must do right. We must never
do wrong. . . .

Evangelicalism, of course, was not simply a late Victorian,
or even indeed a Victorian, religious phenomenon. Its beginnings go back to the eighteenth century, to the Wesleyan
movement. Indeed, as the first of the historians quoted above
has put it: "What most people think of as Victorianism is,
in fact, Wesleyanism or Methodism come to its full fruition,
one of the very few great movements of the modern mind
that has confined itself almost entirely within Anglo-Saxon
limits." But the coincidence of this serious but vital and
dynamic religious faith with the economic potentialities of
industrialism may be regarded as going far to explain the
greatness of the Victorian age.

Perhaps the explanation of the contrasts noted at the beginning of this chapter was in the rise and fall of this great
stream of life. It brought a change of character to the rich
which cannot be denied. A modern historian [2] has said
that during the eighteeneth century "venality in political life
was the counterpart of the coarseness and profligacy of the
social life of the English governing classes" and that there
went with it a quality even more repulsive than venality—
the quality of heartlessness. Men like Wilberforce and
Shaftesbury, the products of Evangelicism, he said, made
"heartlessness unfashionable" and "set an enduring fashion
in respectability which no politician [of the nineteenth cen-
tury] could afford to neglect".

From this new character flowed the social passion which
abolished the slave trade and slavery, reformed the lot of
children in the factories, and set on foot the greatest period
of reform in British history. As our period progressed, the

[2] John Marlowe: *The Puritan Tradition in English Life* (Cresset,
1957).

personal and real impact of this religious challenge began to wane and people began rather to observe moral standards because they were the accepted thing than because they flowed from a real personal experience. Hence the feeling of cramp and hypocrisy, against which people of our own generation have reacted.

The Methodist movement had also awakened the labouring classes who until then had little to do with spiritual things or culture. This had a great influence upon the rise of the trade union and socialist movements in Britain, which unlike those on the Continent were founded in Christian idealism rather than class war and bitterness.

By the time our period opens, Evangelicalism had reached its maximum strength, and was soon to find its position sapped by dangerous influences. But this decline was very gradual, particularly at first; even today Evangelicalism has not disappeared although its teachings are expressed in terms suited to a different age. There was within the church an anglo-catholic alternative to Evangelicalism, stemming from the Oxford Movement of the 1830s. The anglo-catholics put the emphasis on the church as a religious institution—salvation was to be obtained not so much by faith or good works as by Grace, which would come through the sacraments valid only when administered by clergy who had been properly ordained by a bishop. Anglo-catholicism, though popular with many of the clergy, was not something which endangered religion itself, even when it weakened the general hold which the particular Evangelical form of religion had gained over men. Much more dangerous were forces which weakened the hold of religion altogether: such forces were science and pleasure. For science opened up a whole new world and a new way of thinking, and pleasure, made possible in new forms and to a greater extent than ever before by the very success of Victorianism, made the strictness of the Victorian way of life intolerable to a younger generation.

The Challenge of Science: Darwin

Science which explained so many things before unexplained, or wrongly explained, and brought so many new

branches of knowledge into man's view and fuller compre-
hension, which opened up the heavens to observation and
calculation and revealed the laws of physics and chemistry,
and explored the story of the rocks and the biology of animals
and man himself—science was bound to make men think
about their religious beliefs and dogmas. But above all it is
the name of Darwin which is associated with the first great
scientific challenge to religion. Darwin published in 1859 his
On the Origin of Species by Means of Natural Selection, and
in 1871 *The Descent of Man.* Darwin did not himself attack
Christianity, but his theory of evolution—briefly that the different species of animals and man himself were the result of
a long process of evolution and not of a single act of divine
creation—was popularised by the biologist, T. H. Huxley, a
man of culture and literary skill, who developed a fierce
hostility to Christianity or any explanation of life other than
a materialist one. The theory of evolution, so markedly in
contrast with the *Genesis* account of a divine creation of the
world and livings things, became a powerful weapon in the
hands of those who attacked religion. Controversy raged for
many years, and the controversy is not yet still (the teaching
of evolution is forbidden in some American States). On a
famous occasion in 1864, a meeting at Oxford with Bishop
Wilberforce in the chair, Disraeli summed up the essence of
the controversy to his own satisfaction and that of the
Bishop: "The question is this: Is man an ape or an angel?
My Lord, I am on the side of the angels." But neither Disraeli nor Bishop Wilberforce could hold up the tide of
scientific advance. The theory of evolution established itself
and with it, by degrees, a wholly new way of looking at
life: man appeared no longer as a special being created by
God and endowed with a soul but simply as the natural result, like the animals, of a long process of biological development. It was a blow to man's dignity as man; it was a blow to
his faith and to those convictions which had filled and given
meaning to his life.

For Huxley and the materialists science took, as it were,
the place of religion, just as, later on, for some, acceptance
of the Communist ideology of Marx and Lenin was to take
the place of a faith in God. But for some, like Matthew

Arnold, the decline of religion brought "the eternal note of sadness in". In his poem *Dover Beach*, published with *New Poems* in 1867, he, who has been called "the greatest of the Victorian poets", writes of the sea:

> The sea is calm tonight
> The tide is full . . .

and then:

> The Sea of Faith
> Was once, too, at the full, and round earth's shore
> Lay like the folds of a bright girdle furl'd;
> But now I only hear
> Its melancholy, long, withdrawing roar,
> Retreating, to the breath
> Of the night-wind, down the vast edges drear
> And naked shingles of the world . . .

a world which, although to lovers it may seem

> To lie before us like a land of dreams,
> So various, so beautiful, so new,
> Hath really neither joy, nor love, nor light,
> Nor certitude, nor peace, nor help for pain.

Many people effected for themselves some kind of reconciliation between religion and science. Tennyson had written early (in *In Memoriam*, composed between 1833 and 1850 when it was published):

> Let knowledge grow from more to more,
>   But more of reverence in us dwell;
>   That mind and soul, according well,
> May make one music as before,
> But vaster . . .

A Tennyson family diary recorded in 1868: "Mr Darwin called, and seemed to be very kindly, unworldly and agreeable." Tennyson said to him: "Your theory of evolution does not make against Christianity." Darwin answered: "No, certainly not." Tennyson clung to the faith of his youth. In

Crossing the Bar written in his eighty-first year—he died in 1892 at the age of eighty-three—he wrote:

> For tho' from out our bourne of Time and Place
>   The flood may bear me far,
> I hope to see my Pilot face to face
>   When I have crost the bar.

He explained the pilot as "That Divine and Unseen Who is always guiding us", and he told his son to place the poem at the end of all editions of his works.

The Love of Pleasure

Even more dangerous, perhaps, than science to the Evangelical way of life was the new love of pleasure which grew up. Science, though it made a great impact on religious thought and life, offered itself no complete answer to the mystery of life—it only carried further back the ultimate mystery. Indeed, in the 1870s and 1880s a reaction set in: religion was able to accept and, at least partially, reconcile itself to the evolutionary theory, for though evolution could explain the process of life, it did not explain the first cause, or penetrate to the origin of things. Further advances in science revealed a world even more wonderful than the earlier scientists had themselves supposed; fresh discoveries in electricity and in the atomic structure of matter began to cast doubt on the cruder materialist or mechanical theories. Herbert Spencer himself, one of the leaders of the scientific school of thought, maintained in his later writings that behind all the phenomena of the visible world there must be either unknowable mystery or a spiritual power.

But pleasure—perhaps, more accurately, the chasing of pleasure for it own sake—when once awakened, and when once its realisation was made possible more and more widely by late-Victorian material prosperity, was something which would sap the harmony, sobriety and hard work, which were the foundations of the Victorian way of life. In high society the leading influence was that of the Prince of Wales (afterwards Edward VII). He lived a life of easy self-indulgence, very different from that of his mother and late father but

almost identical with that of his grandfathers on both sides.
Though he had been unpopular at first, his charming ways
made him popular later and he was therefore imitated. He
was extravagant in gambling, he began in the eighties to
give dinner parties on Sunday evenings, and he popularised
what has become the modern week-end.

Among the public, novel reading grew in popularity.
Another sign of the desire for light entertainment can be
found in the popularity of the comic operas of Gilbert and
Sullivan. One of the most successful, *The Mikado*, was produced in 1885. During this time, too, was developing the
practice of organised games, which was at first so uniquely
British. Association and rugby football became national institutions in the sixties and seventies, and in association football professionalism came in when soccer matches began to
attract large crowds in the industrial towns. Tennis and golf
became popular a little later, and cycling also.

Literature

In literature, the Victorian age was a distinguished one.
The greatest poets of the nineteenth century—Keats, Shelley,
Byron, Coleridge—were dead some years before Victoria's
accession, though Wordsworth lived on to 1850. But other
notable figures followed on—poets, novelists, men of letters.
The best known novelist and, a little later, the most characteristic thinker, disappeared from the scene soon after our
period opens: Dickens died in 1870, and John Stuart Mill,
the great protagonist of Liberalism and democratic government, in 1873. Three great poets lived on well into the later
Victorian period: Tennyson from 1809 to 1892 and active to
the last, Browning from 1812 to 1889, and Matthew Arnold
from 1822 to 1888, although by about 1870 the best of
their poetry was over. By about that time, also, Swinburne,
Dante Gabriel Rosetti and William Morris—the last two of
whom were also painters—had produced their best work in
poetry. Among the novelists there was Anthony Trollope
(1815–82). *Barchester Towers* had appeared in 1857, but
he went on steadily producing novels until his death. He
worked doggedly with Victorian persistence, rising each

morning at 5.30 a.m. His output was great, as was also his financial success. Hard worker as he was, he enjoyed hunting and whist. And thereafter, there were George Meredith (1828–1909), whose best works were published between 1871 and 1885 when *Diana of the Crossways* appeared, and Thomas Hardy (1840–1928), whose early work was coming out in the seventies to be followed up in 1891 by *Tess of the Durbervilles* and in 1895 by *Jude the Obscure*. Other well-known names are those of R. L. Stevenson—*Treasure Island* in 1883, Rider Haggard—*King Solomon's Mines* in 1885, and the best-seller, Mrs Henry Wood—*East Lynne* had come out in 1861, and with some thirty novels between then and her death in 1887 she achieved a very great total sale. Yet others may be mentioned, Zangwill, Gissing, Kipling (for his short stories), the popular novelists Marie Corelli and Hall Caine, and Mrs Humphry Ward, who appealed to the higher orders of society like Gladstone and the Cecils, and who gave in her novels a clear and detailed picture of how those higher orders lived. At the end of the century another novelist—destined to be famous in the first decades of the next century—was beginning to establish a reputation: H. G. Wells.

At the same time G. Bernard Shaw was publishing plays in book form—the Victorian age was a poor period in the theatre. It was not until the first decades of the next century that a revival in the theatre put Shaw's plays on the stage and established him as a dramatist with an international reputation. At the end of the nineteenth century also new poets were appearing—Kipling and Thomas Hardy were poets as well as prose writers, and there were Robert Bridges, W. B. Yeats and A. E. Housman, whose *A Shropshire Lad* appeared in 1896.

The last decade of the nineteenth century has been called the "naughty nineties". The puritanism of the earlier decades gave place to something more fickle. This was the period of the brilliant but morally decadent Oscar Wilde (1856–1900) who set himself up as an apostle of "art for art's sake". *The Picture of Dorian Gray* expressed his sentiments in novel form. His wit showed itself in his plays which had a success on the stage between 1892 and 1895 (e.g. *Lady Win-*

dermere's Fan and *The Importance of Being Earnest*). His moral failings led to two years in prison and his *Ballad of Reading Gaol*. This was the period also of the *Yellow Book*, a periodical fashionable at the time, which along with poetry and *belles-lettres* published the clever drawings of Aubrey Beardsley. There was talk of decadence and *fin-de-siècle*— but much of this was a pose, and the decadent movement in art and letters had no lasting influence in the history of literature.

Newspapers: A Change of Character

Much more important because enduring in its effect was a radical change which took place in the newspaper press. The heavy character of Victorian writing was apparent in the newspapers. If a modern reader will turn up the files of *The Times* of Victorian days he will find them stodgy and forbidding. But their tone was serious and dignified, and the journalists wrote with a sense of responsibility. They sought to appeal to educated and intelligent readers, who were to be found in the upper and middle classes. Now, however, a new and much larger class of readers was growing up—men, and women also, given elementary education by the Board schools of the 1870 Education Act. Their education was but slight, and they would have neither inclination nor time enough to tackle heavy reading. To meet their need, and to profit by it, a new, popular press was created—the *Daily Mail* in 1896, the *Daily Express* in 1900, and the *Daily Mirror* in 1904.

A combination of sensationalism and commercialism brought large circulations for the popular dailies. The idea of a popular press sprang from George Newnes' success with *Tit-Bits*, a weekly he had started in 1880. The secret was to provide for the new class of readers for whom the existing newspapers with lengthy articles, built up of long solid paragraphs, and calling for application and thought in their reading, were quite unsuitable, or at least were unattractive and would go unread. The weekly, in contrast, consisted of short articles, as far as possible in story form, and with words, sentences, paragraphs all short and easily to be grasped. To increase the effect of his paper he added prize competitions, and free insurance against railway accidents. In his office he had a young man called Alfred Harmsworth. This young man eventually came out as a rival, with another paper, *Answers*, and with his brother Harold achieved success and wealth. Later they entered daily journalism by launching the *Daily Mail* as a halfpenny paper, whereas most of the existing dailies cost one penny, and *The Times* threepence. (There were, indeed, two London dailies in existence which cost a halfpenny, but neither had secured a large circulation.)

The *Daily Mail*, however, was an immediate success; in three years time it reached a circulation of 543,000, more than double that of any other daily. With this spectacular achievement the new daily made a revolution in the newspaper world—it might indeed be said that it marked the popularisation of the newspaper world. The Harmsworths achieved wealth and power (Alfred became Lord Northcliffe in 1907, bought *The Times* in 1908, and Harold became Lord Rothermere in 1913), but these were their interests and objects rather than informing and guiding the public mind. The biographer of Northcliffe has described his powers and their limitations:

Boyish the limited range of his intellect, which seldom concerns itself with anything but the immediate, the obvious, the popular. Boyish his irresponsibility, his disinclination to take himself or his publications seriously; his conviction that whatever benefits them is justifiable, and that it is not his business to consider the effect of their contents on the public mind.

The first issue of the *Daily Mail* (May 4th, 1896) carried close to the title the slogan: "The Busy Man's Daily Journal." And this was, perhaps, the key to its success—it aimed at being concise and compact, and giving the busy man and the business man a quick view of the news which he could take in, almost at a glance, on his journey to work. It was of manageable size—eight pages, and slightly smaller pages, compared with the eighteen of *The Times,* and it cut down the mass of advertisements; its church, law and company reports were briefer than those of *The Times*; and, above all, its news paragraphs were short and many, instead of being lengthy, solid articles. *The Daily Mail* sub-editors had been trained (for some weeks before the paper appeared publicly) to avoid verbosity. Before 1896 newspapers had commonly printed the news reports as they came in from the agencies, importance being judged by length. Now the news was sub-edited and arranged to make a more immediate impact on the reader's mind. In addition, the new daily contained a serial story, and a magazine section—"an entirely new feature in modern journalism"—with a "Woman's Realm" ("Today's Dinner", "A New Bonnet" and "Hints for Housewives"). Behind all this, as the new paper explained, there was the latest printing machinery—the new linotype setting machine. This effected a big economy in production, and enabled the paper to sell at half the usual price.

The reader of today, nevertheless, if he should come across an early issue of the *Daily Mail,* would find its appearance old-fashioned—so much further have the tendencies started then been carried since. Then the front and back pages of the *Mail* were covered with advertisements just as were the front and back of *The Times*. The reader could not pick up an immediate impression of the day's news from the headlines on the front page of the popular daily as he does today.

But on the news pages, inside, the headlines of the new paper were larger and more lurid than those of the established papers. It is interesting to compare the treatment given to some great events by *The Times* and the *Daily Mail*. Look, for example, at the fall of Omdurman in 1898:

The Times	September 3rd	*Daily Mail*
Latest Intelligence		Omdurman Captured
Fall of Omdurman		Two Desperate Battles fought
Complete Defeat of the		before the City Walls
Dervishes		Khalif's Army utterly routed
Flight of the Khalifa		Thousands of Dervishes killed
		and wounded—Serious
		British Losses
		Superb Charge of the 21st
		Lancers

Magnificent Heroism of the
Doomed Dervishes

and the relief of Mafeking in 1900:

The Times	May 19th	*Daily Mail*

Latest Intelligence
  The War
Relief of Mafeking
The Siege abandoned
Entry of British Forces

Relief of Mafeking
The Besiegers' Cordon broken
  by the Flying Column
Heavy Bombardment and Flight
  of the Boers
The Unknown British Force
  triumphantly enters the Town
Unparalleled Scenes of
  Rejoicing

Whereas *The Times* having given about half its page to this big item then devoted the rest of the page to the ordinary news, the *Daily Mail* printed a column headed "London's Roar of Jubilation" followed by sub-headings, "Wild Frenzy that Surpasses Description", "Lord Mayor speaks to a vast shouting Multitude", "Thousands Serenade Mrs Baden-Powell", and lower down another column headed "Country's Chorus of Joy" with a number of small items entitled "Plymouth Illuminated", "Bradford's Buzzers Sounded", "How York Felt", "Nottingham's Colours", "Glasgow Declares Holiday", "Brighton's Parade", and "Belfast Lights its Torches".

Good and bad were mixed in the new papers. "Written by office boys for office boys", Lord Salisbury said of them. But there were, of course, great advantages in an attractive lay-out, clear headings and manageable paragraphs. But the sensationalism of the new press was to be deplored, as was also the great power which the larger circulation gave to owners who might be irresponsible. The new press, however, had come to stay. Beside appealing to many of the slightly educated poor, it appealed also to many people in the business classes, for at this time there were larger numbers of business men who had had no secondary education. It caught, too, the attention of women, by tradition and up-bringing with a smaller interest in politics and public affairs than men, in all classes of society. But the change does represent a decline from the high standards of the previous period. Like religion and literature, the press also was marked by a falling away from the highest standards of the Evangelicalism which had imparted its moral fervour to the age of Victoria.

Things were changing—slowly, often imperceptibly to those living at the time, but clearly enough to the historian who can look back and compare one period with another. Families were smaller; upper and middle class parents were beginning to practise birth control, although among the working classes families of nine or ten children were still common. Women were beginning to claim equality with men— for example, the right of the married woman to her own property (Acts passed in 1882 and 1893), the privilege of school and university education, and the vote. Much of the spirit and character of what we think of as Victorian passed naturally from the Victorian into the Edwardian age, but as the years went on there were new problems, new anxieties, new challenges.

6

Liberalism Triumphant

QUEEN VICTORIA'S REIGN was the longest in British history, and when she died on January 22nd, 1901, her death seemed to mark the end of an epoch; the nation had already passed from the nineteenth into the twentieth century, and now the great Victorian age itself had come to a close. During her reign wealth, prosperity and national power had vastly increased. Britain had held a position of high authority and influence in international affairs, and for long periods had maintained the *Pax Britannica*; statesmen and people had been touched by a feeling of national greatness and imperial mission (Joseph Chamberlain was the last minister to see the Queen—she who had once hated his early republicanism and radical policies; now he had become her much admired minister, the great imperialist, who could describe the Queen as "the greatest of Englishwomen"); men and women were moved in political affairs as in their domestic life by the teachings and sentiment of Evangelicalism— of all this the grand old Queen had become the symbol, giving an example to her people and at the same time reflecting their basic and characteristic thoughts and feelings. There was a hush of sorrow and mourning over Britain and the Empire: the passing of the Queen might well mark the end of a period of greatness, and the uncertain future stretched ahead with its own new problems and the consequent troubles and storms the signs of which were already to be seen. The Boer War was not over; there was the social problem at home with the menace of class conflict; there was the problem of Ireland; and there was, in foreign affairs, the danger of Britain's isolation and the growing threat of German military power.

If men looked back they could see the wonderful scientific and technical developments which had been made during the Queen's reign, above all, perhaps, the development of railways. The year after her accession to the throne the main line railway was opened between London and Birmingham; during her reign the railway network spread throughout the country, and other networks and great continental routes were created in Europe and America. The railway was a British invention; the motor car, at the end of Victoria's reign, was a German invention, and the first cars were made in France. This was indicative of the great change in the industrial sphere: Britain was no longer alone and supreme, for inventors were busy in other countries also and industrialists were ready to exploit and develop their inventions. Not only were the first motor cars running towards the end of Victoria's reign, but the telephone and electricity were coming into use, Marconi was sending the first "wireless" messages, and a few years later, in 1903, the first aeroplane flight was made by the Wright brothers in America. The first air crossing of the English Channel was made in 1909 by the Frenchman Blériot. There were, indeed, remarkable achievements—but how much more was to come. The Queen had reigned for over sixty years: in that period what would have seemed in 1901 to be some of the greatest advances of all times had been made. But what a short way ahead men could see: in the next sixty years came radio, air transport all over the world, television, atomic power, and the first journeys into space by the Russian and American spacemen.

Balfour Follows Lord Salisbury: The Education Act of 1902

In 1901, however, all this was far ahead. The Conservative Party—still under the "venerable, august Lord Salisbury, Prime Minister since God knew when", as Winston Churchill put it later, was in power. On his retirement in the following year, his nephew, Balfour, became Prime Minister. Balfour carried a most important educational measure, important because it was high time for educational advance. Elementary schools paid for by public money had been provided by the Education Act of 1870, but England lagged behind Germany and France, for the government had not provided schools supplying the next stage in education. It was this need which was now met. The Education Act of 1902 provided secondary schools, which were to be paid for, as in the case of the existing elementary schools, out of the local rates with the help of grants from the central government. At the same time the Act did a lot to simplify the very complicated system of educational administration—"administrative muddle", as it has been called. Three years earlier the Board of Education had been created, with its head, President of the Board, a member of the government. (Forty-two years later the President was to become Minister of Education.) The Board replaced three different educational authorities at the centre. The Act of 1902 abolished the School Boards, created in 1870, and transferred their functions to the new local authorities, the County Councils and County Borough (i.e., large towns) Councils. Thus the local authorities were to control both elementary and secondary education, and were to use the rates to maintain the voluntary schools as well and were to have a large measure of control over them.

Extraordinary as it seems nowadays this very reasonable Act was the cause of a bitter political and religious conflict. As a Conservative bill it was fiercely denounced inside and outside parliament by Lloyd George. Outside parliament the bill was attacked by the Nonconformists largely because the rates were now to be used to support Church of England elementary schools as well as the local authority schools (a not very plausible objection for the taxes had long been used for this purpose). The Nonconformists urged passive resistance to the Act, and in some cases individuals refused to pay rates and in Wales some of the local authorities refused to operate the Act. Nothing came of this opposition, however, and after the Liberal victory of 1906 the government failed—in face of House of Lord's opposition—to pass a new bill of their own. And some years later a great Liberal

statesman and educationalist, H. A. L. Fisher, could write:
"So much educational progress has been accomplished under
the Act of 1902 that much of the criticism then levelled
against it from the Liberal benches seems now to be lacking
in perspective."

The Act was indeed of fundamental importance as the
second great stage in creating a national system of education. It brought into existence what was known as the "educational ladder". For it was now possible for the clever child
of poor parents to pass from the elementary school (which
was free) to the secondary school by winning a scholarship
or free place, and to go on thence by means of scholarships
or grants to the universities, for new universities had
also been created during the nineteenth century (at first by
private benefaction, aided later by the state) in addition to
the two older ones of Oxford and Cambridge. The general
structure of the educational system was to remain the same
until after the Second World War.

Chamberlain and Imperial Preference

The Education Act of 1902 had proved a means of rallying the Liberals (divided by the Boer War) against the government. Something which did even more for the Liberals
was Joseph Chamberlain's tariff reform campaign. For Chamberlain who had once split the Liberal Party over home rule
for Ireland was soon to split the Conservative Party over
tariff reform. Although not Prime Minister, Chamberlain was
in some ways the outstanding Englishman of his time. Winston Churchill (recently elected Conservative M.P. for Old-
ham) thought of him as "incomparably the most live, spar-
kling, insurgent, compulsive figure in British affairs". *The
Times* had written of the Colonial Secretary: "Amongst his
countrymen beyond the seas he enjoys—and deservedly enjoys—a popularity greater than any other imperial statesman has ever commanded." But his splendid vision of Empire would not let him rest—he was dissatisfied with progress
made, and his driving energy was forcing him to look for
new and more effective policies. The result of the fourth
Colonial Conference in 1902 had been a great disappointment to Chamberlain; the colonial premiers—in spite of

their co-operation in the Boer War, which had actually made them more conscious of their own national existence than of the Empire—were deaf to his arguments for an Empire Council and for larger contributions to common imperial defence. Only in the matter of trade did they prove more Empire-minded, and they looked towards imperial preference.

Chamberlain's mind, therefore, turned in this direction. He thought of imperial preference and Empire development going on hand in hand: the resources of the Empire would be developed and made available to the whole Empire and gradually reduced in cost as production increased—and all this would go on behind a defensive tariff against the outside world with a preferential reduction in favour of Empire goods. In May 1903, Chamberlain proclaimed in speeches in Birmingham and in the House of Commons that he abandoned free trade in favour of imperial preference. Though many rank and file Conservatives supported Chamberlain's views, the older leaders opposed them—so firmly had free trade come to be accepted by both parties. Thus the Conservative Party was split—desperately did Balfour seek some reconciling formula: perhaps they could agree to differ, or perhaps tariffs might be used but only for purposes of retaliation to force down foreign tariffs.

But Chamberlain resigned from the government in order to be free to lead his new campaign. This caused dismissals and other resignations, and Balfour had to reconstruct his government. Meanwhile Chamberlain, backed by the Tariff Reform League, was fighting a large-scale campaign. As the struggle went on it became less one for the Empire and imperial preference and more one for protection for its own sake. Asquith followed Chamberlain about the country answering his protectionist arguments with the powerful arguments for free trade. Popular feeling was afraid of the food taxes which an Empire fiscal policy must mean; Chamberlain's strong line was that tariffs would keep out foreign goods and give employment to all at home.

The Liberal Government of 1905: Campbell-Bannerman

The attack on free trade rallied all the Liberals, and al-

Hap Chamberlain, coup in might have never had labor party (handwritten annotation)

though Balfour early in 1905 was able to effect a reunion between his followers and the Chamberlainites, the government was under heavy pressure. Another issue brought it great unpopularity—it had agreed to the English authorities in South Africa bringing indentured Chinese coolies into the South African mines. For this there was a strong economic argument. Labour was short, and the Chinese workers would enable the Rand mine-owners to make larger profits and provide increased revenue for the annexed territories. But the Chinese were virtual slaves working underground and confined to compounds. This miserable business infuriated humane and liberal people, and counted much against the Conservative government. These pressures combined to make Balfour resign in December 1905. He did not dissolve parliament, but left the Liberals to form a government, hoping that in doing so their recent wartime divisions would be increased by the added difficulties of the Irish home rule question which had been recently raised again. Balfour proved wrong: Campbell-Bannerman formed an impressive Liberal government, and the elections of 1906 gave his party a sweeping victory. Birmingham remained loyal to Chamberlain, but the Liberal victory, in effect, marked his end, for in July he was struck by paralysis and could take no further part in politics. It was a tragic end to a great career—how much more might have been achieved if things had gone a little differently. "Had there been no home rule split and had he succeeded Gladstone as Liberal premier, social reform might have come in England nearly twenty years sooner than it did. In that case the Labour party—at least in the form which it actually took—might never have been born." [1]

Campbell-Bannerman, the Liberal Prime Minister, had served as Secretary for War under Gladstone and Lord Rosebery. He was not a fluent speaker, but he had become, nevertheless, leader of the party in the House of Commons in 1898. He was rich, well-liked, unselfish in party loyalty, and came to show qualities of shrewdness and strong purpose which marked him out for the highest office. Like Gladstone also, as he had grown older, he had moved to the left, and

[1] R. C. K. Ensor: *England 1870–1914*, p. 389.

so was ready to lead the ardent reforming party which the 1906 election brought to parliament. He had been able, too, to smooth over the differences between the Liberal imperialists and the pro-Boers in the party. His government had in it a remarkable number of able men: there were Asquith as Chancellor of the Exchequer, Grey as Foreign Secretary, Haldane as Secretary for War; there were John Morley, Bryce, and John Burns (of the London Docks strike but now a Liberal); the radical Lloyd George entered the cabinet as President of the Board of Trade; among those in junior places were Reginald McKenna, Herbert Samuel, Walter Runciman and Winston Churchill (who had recently left the Conservatives on the free trade issue).

The elections of January 1906, fought largely on the issues of tariff reform and Chinese labour, gave the Liberal Party 377 seats with a majority of 84 over all other parties combined. The Conservatives (with the Liberal Unionists) won 157 seats, the Irish Nationalists 83, and, smaller in number but more sensational, there were 53 Labour members. Of these 29 were elected under the auspices of the Labour Representation Committee, while the rest, though not yet under this body, were to join three years later what had now become the new Labour Party. The sweeping victory which the Liberal Party had won gave it easy and assured control of the Commons. But the Conservatives had a permanent majority in the House of Lords, and as events were to show (and also correspondence between Balfour and the Conservative leader in the Lords) they were ready to use it to block Liberal bills. The use of this power was to provoke a bitter constitutional conflict, a conflict which was in effect the last struggle of the aristocracy against domination (as they saw it) by the people, of the danger of which the presence in the House of the Labour members and Lloyd George and many of the Liberals was the sign.

The first task—and C.-B.'s greatest triumph—was the settlement of South Africa. The recruiting of Chinese labour was stopped at once. Then the Premier proceeded to introduce self-government into the conquered Boer states—he could do this by letters patent and did not need a bill which the Lords would have thrown out, for there was bitter Conservative opposition. Elections in the Transvaal brought in General Botha as Prime Minister with General Smuts as his deputy. Both worked for reconciliation, and became strong friends of Britain. The task of reconstructing South Africa went on, although Campbell-Bannerman himself did not live to see its completion. A Convention met at Durban in October 1908, and delegates from the four South African parliaments worked out a constitution for South Africa. In the following autumn the necessary bill passed the British parliament—for by now the Conservatives were won over by the obvious success of conciliatory measures—and it came into force in 1910.

The work of government is many-sided, and there were many other tasks. The government was fortunate in having in its War Minister, Haldane, a man who understood the danger from Germany and was determined upon army reform—though he had to contend with the peaceful inclinations of Liberals generally and the desire of the cabinet for economy in particular. Haldane, who had many contacts with Germany, was fully aware of that country's military might and of the power of its industry and science. His principal work was to create a general staff for the army, and to organise an Expeditionary Force of six infantry divisions and one cavalry division, ready to be rapidly mobilised and sent abroad if necessary. In another field, the government was harassed by ardent feminists. During the early years of the Liberal government the militant suffragette movement grew in size and activity: these women activists demanded the vote for women and drew attention to their demand by interrupting political meetings and padlocking themselves to railings. Change was going on, too, in Empire affairs. The Colonial Conference of 1907 decided that the term "Dominions" be used in future in place of "Colonies" for the self-governing territories, indicating the growing consciousness of their separate power and nationhood.

Meanwhile a new star was shining ever more brightly in the political firmament. Lloyd George began to show that he was not only an orator and devastating critic but also a constructive statesman. Born in 1863, he was educated at a Welsh elementary school, and by his uncle, Richard Lloyd, shoemaker and Baptist pastor, who devoted himself to bringing up the boy; he had enjoyed none of the advantages of birth and wealth but, becoming a solicitor and entering parliament, had made his way as a result of native wit, brilliance and perseverance. He had carried two measures which did not rouse party issues, a Merchant Shipping Act in 1906, and a Patents Act in 1907. He was successful in settling two serious labour disputes, one with the railwaymen and the other with shipyard engineers. And he was instrumental in clearing up the chaos of private dock companies in London and creating a single Port of London Authority.

Asquith's Government—Asquith and Lloyd George

When Campbell-Bannerman died in April 1908, Asquith (Home Secretary under Gladstone in 1892) became Prime Minister, bringing Lloyd George into his place as Chancellor of the Exchequer. Years later, in a mood of reminiscence, Lloyd George said: "Do you know, Asquith followed the policy of Gladstone when selecting men for his Cabinet. He made his choice according to the college which a man went to. Asquith, however, was never consistent, for had he been so, I would never have been a member of his Cabinet, or," and L.G. laughed, "was it that he was misinformed about my college?" There was an interesting and enlightening comparison there. Asquith (born in 1852) had also come of Nonconformist, Congregationalist stock, but of a more substantial middle-class Yorkshire textile family. Not rich, Asquith, too, suffered the loss of his father at an early age. Helped by relations, however, he was sent to the City of London School, and won a scholarship to Balliol. At Oxford he had a brilliant career and was President of the Union, which gave him a lifelong sentiment for Oxford. After the University he built up a substantial practice as a barrister. Lloyd George rose without these advantages—he remained at heart the son of the Welsh village, the spokesman of Wales and of Welsh Nonconformity.

Asquith was a man of powerful intellect, a good speaker, precise, exact and logical in argument, of great dignity, more effective in the House of Commons than outside. He was lacking, perhaps, in imagination, but was an excellent man of affairs, able to carry on the government from day to day with skill and mastery. It was said of him that "he treated all questions with the cheery calm and assurance of an experienced man of business, whose good health and excellent nerves were steeled by devotion to the game of golf". Lloyd George, on the other hand, was a man of dynamic energy, imagination, personality. He, too, enjoyed good health, was calm and possessed of good nerves at times of crisis: he, too, played golf—but he had flair, charm and a Celtic magic in his heart and at his fingers' end, a magic which made itself felt in the gestures which adorned his speeches. He was an orator of outstanding powers, who could command not only reason and fact, but the great masses up and down the country, and who could fill them with zest, fervour and inspiration.

Social Reform, the Budget and the Parliament Act

Now begins the great work of social reform for which the government of Asquith is chiefly remembered and with which the name of Lloyd George is so closely associated—the work which laid the foundations of what today is known as the welfare state. People were moving steadily—if slowly—away from the older ideas of individualism and *laissez faire*, which had pictured every man working for himself and being entirely responsible for himself and his own family. Poverty and the existence of slums all went to show that sometimes the government must help; at least special aid must be given to the old and the sick, to those unable to help themselves. First came old age pensions. In the Budget of 1908—which Asquith, although now Prime Minister, presented himself, for he had framed it while still Chancellor of the Exchequer—the necessary money was allocated. Lloyd George handled the further stages of the Budget and the piloting of the Old Age Pensions Bill through the Commons. Such provision for old age had been long talked of and so the ground was prepared. The bill passed both Houses, although in the Lords some alarm was voiced lest the pensions should discourage thrift. The small pension of 5s. per week was non-contributory, and was to begin at age seventy; it was only intended for the really poor, and therefore there was a means test. But the pension was undoubtedly a boon to many who came to know it as their "Lloyd George".

Further measures to deal with poverty came from Churchill and as a result of the researches of the economist W. H. Beveridge. As Home Secretary, Churchill passed in 1909 his Trade Boards Act to prevent "sweating". In some industries, notably cheap tailoring, the workers were miserably underpaid, and the Act, which was later much extended, made a start by setting up trade boards to fix the wages in certain industries. In the same year, as a result of the work Beveridge had put into his book *Unemployment* which showed that very often it was the casual labourers who were unemployed, an Act was passed setting up Labour Exchanges all over the country. Their purpose was to provide information about jobs available, and Beveridge was appointed to organise them.

Lloyd George was, of course, thinking of more and wider policies of social reform. He was considering a system of social insurance, and he wanted to disestablish the Anglican Church in Nonconformist Wales (later achieved by an Act passed before the Great War, but not coming into force until after it). But before anything more could be achieved a struggle with the House of Lords would be necessary—they had thrown out in 1908 a licensing Bill to restrict the drink trade although the King had urged the unwisdom of the rejection and the bishops had supported the bill. And things were not going too well for the Liberals outside parliament. Trade was bad and the party was losing by-elections. There were also international difficulties, chief of which was the growing threat to British naval supremacy by the building of dreadnoughts in Germany. The laying down of German dreadnoughts—though the original *Dreadnought* was British —meant that the programme of British building must be expanded and accelerated. "We want eight, and we won't wait", became a music hall refrain. Eight new dreadnoughts meant that fifteen million pounds must be raised by additional taxation. This gave Lloyd George the opportunity in his Budget of 1909 to bring in new taxes to tax the rich, and at the same time to launch a struggle against the House of Lords on an important issue which could be calculated to revive the flagging popular fortunes of Liberalism. It was a clever piece of political strategy.

Thus taxes were increased, and super-tax was introduced, but the most novel element was the proposed duties on Land Values. There was to be a duty on what was known as the unearned increment of land value (i.e., the increase in the value of land, not brought about by the owner, but caused by the development of the district by society) and also a tax on the capital value of undeveloped land and minerals. To establish the value of land it would be necessary to make a valuation of all the land of Britain, and this aroused strong opposition from landowners. What the income from the new taxes might have been is a matter of dispute, for they were never fully put into operation and some ten years later were abandoned. But at the time the new duties stirred up violent political controversy: the landlord class with the House of Lords as their instrument attacked L.G.'s proposals, and the people supported him.

Lloyd George made some great speeches up and down the country at this time, attacking the peers as wealthy monopolists unwilling to pay for national defence and social insurance. A fierce attack on the landed interests he made at Limehouse was long remembered, and in a speech in Newcastle he asked:

> Who ordained that a few should have the land of Britain as a perquisite? Who made ten thousand people owners of the soil and the rest of us trespassers on the land of our birth? Who is responsible for the scheme of things whereby one man is engaged through life in grinding labour to win a bare and precarious subsistence . . . and another man who does not toil receives every hour of the day, every hour of the night, whilst he slumbers, more than his poor neighbour receives in a whole year of toil? . . . These are the questions that will be asked. The answers are charged with peril for the order of things the Peers represent, but they are fraught with rare and refreshing fruit for the parched lips of the multitude who have been treading the dusty road along which the people have marched through the dark ages and are now emerging into the light.

Not surprisingly the abuse of Lloyd George by those he attacked was equally strong. Churchill came in for abuse also for, although he was the grandson of a duke, he became president of the Budget League formed to support the proposals of his friend L.G. "I should like," said one duke, "to see Winston Churchill and Lloyd George in the middle of twenty couple of dog hounds."

At the end of November 1909, the Lords rejected the Budget. This was a breach of the Constitution, of the practice which for many years had been generally accepted of control over finance by the House of Commons. A general election followed in January 1910, and the Liberals won, but with a majority dependent on Irish and Labour support, which was, however, forthcoming as both groups were ready to limit the House of Lords' veto and to give Ireland home rule. The Liberals were determined to deal with the Lords, and brought in their Parliament Bill. Now the Lords allowed the Budget to go through. On May 6th, unexpectedly, King Edward VII died. The new King, George V, tried to bring about a party truce. The politicians felt they would like to give the new monarch a peaceful start, and as a result a constitutional conference met (with four representatives of each of the two great parties), but it failed to agree. Lloyd George's powerful and original mind was shown, meanwhile, in proposals he made, with Asquith's support, for a coalition with the Conservatives to reach an agreed policy on the outstanding issues: House of Lords, Irish Home Rule, social reform, and even tariff policy. Balfour liked the idea, as did some other Conservative leaders. But the proposal came to nothing, and the party struggle was resumed, for many Conservatives were quite unwilling to work with L.G. A second election, in December, produced almost the same result as before. At last, in August 1911, after long debates and bitter struggles, and faced with the prospect of a large creation of peers if they did not pass the Bill, the House of Lords allowed it to pass and the Parliament Bill became law. The House of Lords lost its power of veto: in future finance measures were exempt from their veto, and other measures could be held up but not for more than two years. Thus, at last, the door was open for more radical Liberal measures.

Most important was Lloyd George's National Insurance Bill.

But among a number of measures during 1911 some others are also worth recalling: there was a Shops Act, establishing the principle of a weekly half-holiday, there was an Official Secrets Act (a sign of growing German espionage), and the payment of M.P.'s was introduced—this latter had long been a minor aim of Liberals but the financial difficulties of the Labour members made the matter urgent.

Lloyd George had introduced his National Insurance Bill while the Parliament Bill was still in the Commons, and when it had become law it was possible in the autumn of 1911 to pass National Insurance. National Insurance was, above all, the work of Lloyd George himself, whereas the Parliament Act had been the special responsibility of the Prime Minister. L.G. had studied the German model, and had visited Germany to make enquiries at first hand, for there sickness and accident insurance and old age pensions had existed since the days of Bismarck. A British workman, before the days of Lloyd George, if he fell sick and could not go to work, lost his wages, and his family would be likely to suffer from hunger; it was likely also that the workman would be unable to pay for the services of a doctor. The new insurance system provided sick pay, i.e., money for maintenance, during sickness, and also free medical attention and medicine. The new scheme was a contributory one, and, in addition to covering the whole working population against sickness, it also covered those working in certain industries, e.g., building and engineering, against unemployment. Compulsory contributions were collected from workman and employer by means of a stamped card, the workman paying 4d., the employer 3d., and the government adding 2d. The scheme was complicated—for a certain amount of working-class insurance had been done for some time by the friendly societies and trade unions. But L.G. was successful in winning their support and using them as "approved societies" to administer the money payments under the scheme. He was not so successful in winning over the doctors to accept his scheme of a panel of doctors in each district who would undertake medical treatment under the scheme—but eventually enough were willing to accept the scheme to make it a success.

National Insurance passed through Parliament largely be-

1 QUEEN VICTORIA

2 W. E. GLADSTONE

3 LORD SALISBURY

4 BENJAMIN DISRAELI

5 Slums in London about 1870

6 The Great Dock Strike, London, 1889

7 CHARLES STEWART PARNELL

8 DAVID LLOYD GEORGE

9 KEIR HARDIE
From a contemporary cartoon

10 JOSEPH CHAMBERLAIN

11 The Grand Fleet
in the North Sea

YOUR COUNTRY NEEDS

YOU

12 Kitchener's
recruiting poster

13 Trench warfare in
the First World War

18 Churchill, Roosevelt, and Stalin at Yalta in the Crimea,
February 1945

19 The United Nations Building, New York

20 The Polaris missile being launched from a submerged submarine off Cape Canaveral, Florida

21 Astronaut Colonel John Glenn on the way to his space capsule, February 1962

cause it was known that, if the Lords rejected it, it would nevertheless in due course become law under the Parliament Act. Nor did the Conservative leaders wish to oppose the principle of social reform—but they detested the man and the party who were carrying this particular measure. Outside in the country, however, there was bitter opposition to Lloyd George's bill. Many workmen did not like having to pay their contributions. There was particular opposition, too, to the idea of mistresses having to lick stamps to stick on the cards of domestic servants. "What, me lick stamps?" exclaimed an angry duchess in a popular cartoon. *The Daily Mail* led a violent campaign on this issue, and organised an Albert Hall meeting. Lloyd George, however, was more than the equal of his opponents, though his "9d. for 4d." argument seemed to some people rather near to a bribing of the electorate. The exaggerated and sensational character of the campaign was not healthy for democracy. Yet today it is clear that Lloyd George was the great pioneer of social insurance in this country: his unemployment provisions had to be vastly extended after the First World War, and after the Second, on the lines of the Beveridge *Report,* national health insurance was expanded into a comprehensive system of social insurance and health service.

The Trade Unions

Apart from social reform (and Lloyd George at one time or another had been considering the nationalisation of the railways and a great scheme of land reform—"to free the land that is to this very hour shackled with the chains of feudalism") the years 1905 to 1914 were a time of ferment and excitement in other fields also. The advent of the Labour Party in parliament encouraged the trade unions to press their demands on the Liberal government. In spite of previous trade union legislation, the unions were still faced by certain dangers. For example, in the Taff Vale Case of 1900, the judges decided that a union's funds were liable for civil damages, i.e., that a union might have to pay for damages suffered by an employer due to a strike. The Trades Disputes Act of 1906 put this right and gave the unions a strong position in that, in future, they could not be sued for damages of this kind. Later another kind of difficulty arose. A judge decided (the Osborne judgment 1908) that a union could only lawfully use its funds for union, not for political, purposes—a decision which had contributed to acceptance in parliament of the payment of M.P.s. In 1913 the Liberal government, then dependent on Labour support for its majority, passed the Trade Union Act which allowed unions to make a political levy for such purposes as paying elections expenses and salaries to trade union M.Ps. The levy was to be collected by the union, unless a member formally disagreed, "contracting-out", as it was called. This Act enabled the unions to give more powerful financial backing to the Labour Party.

During these years, too, there was a movement among the unions for direct action, encouraged partly by the Osborne judgment which had cut them off from political activities, partly by the idea of class war to be waged by the trade unions against employers, and even against the government, by means of strikes. Direct action was also the working class counterpart to the House of Lords' veto. "If the peers," the unions could say, "may sabotage the constitution for their own purposes, why may not we?" There was a wave of strikes in 1910—some against official union advice—and serious rioting for three days among the miners of Tonypandy, in South Wales, to which troops had to be sent. In 1911, after a lull, there were more strikes: troops had to fire on dockers in Liverpool, and two men were killed; a general railway strike followed, and troops were encamped in the London parks; and in Llanelly rioting broke out and troops fired, several men being killed. Lloyd George was called in as negotiator, and managed to settle the disputes. In 1912 there were strikes of miners and dockers—but eventually the movement petered out.

Suffragettes

Akin to the working-class movement of direct action was that of the militant suffragettes, who carried on a campaign of violence to draw attention to their demand for votes for women. They interrupted political meetings, broke windows, and, when in prison, went on hunger strike which led to their forcible feeding through tubes. Lloyd George and many of the Liberals were in favour of votes for women, but nevertheless the Government was not successful in passing a measure which would satisfy them; not unnaturally M.P.s were exasperated by the women's activities. The suffragettes intensified their campaign (organised by Christabel Pankhurst, living in Paris): houses were burned down, fires were started in pillar-boxes, bombs exploded. In 1913 the "Cat and Mouse" Act gave the authorities the upper hand: hunger strikers could be released—to avoid their dying in prison— but re-arrested when necessary.

Ireland Again: Home Rule Passes in 1914

Most serious of all the threats to the democratic conduct of affairs by the Government was the dangerous situation which developed in Ireland. In 1912 a bill for giving home rule to Ireland was introduced: the Irish Nationalists had long pressed for this, and now the Parliament Act made its success possible. The British parliament at Westminster was to remain supreme, but there would be a separate parliament for Ireland in Dublin. The auspices were more favourable than ever before: the land problem had been largely solved as a result of successive British legislation starting with Gladstone; the leader of the Irish Nationalists, John Redmond, was a moderate man and well disposed to England; the success of reconciliation and self-government in South Africa encouraged Liberals to think of making Redmond "the Irish Botha".

But, in effect, the proposal for Irish home rule divided Ireland into two armed camps. The protestant opposition was stronger now; Belfast, with its important shipbuilding, was a larger city than Dublin, and the Ulstermen's feelings hardened into a determination not to submit to Dublin rule. A leading lawyer, Sir Edward Carson, though born in Dublin, became Ulster's leader, and he had strong support from Bonar Law, who had followed Balfour as leader of the Conservative Party. Carson and Bonar Law took the salute at a review, early in 1912, of the Ulster Volunteers. Next, the Irish in the south started to arm and drill (though this was against the will of Redmond). Thus, what were really two private armies came into existence, the Conservative Party giving strong assistance to Ulster, the Liberals backing the Irish Nationalists. There was a danger of civil war in Ireland. Worse still, many officers in the British Army, which included a number of Ulstermen, sympathised with Ulster. A brigadier and a number of officers, in what was known as the Curragh Mutiny, offered their resignations rather than coerce Ulster—and the government (with the foreign situation in view) dared not take strong action against the army. In the summer of 1914, the Home Rule Bill passed the House of Commons for the third time. Meanwhile, desperate attempts at compromise were going on, including the proposal to exclude Ulster from the home rule provision. A conference met —including Asquith and Lloyd George, Bonar Law, Carson and Redmond—but they failed to agree. Then came war in Europe, the First World War, and the Irish problem was put aside for the time. The lesser menace was put into the shadow by the greater. After four years of slaughter and the troubles which followed, it would not be long before men were looking back on the pre-war period as a golden age, recalling the security and freedom of those times, the great country houses, the London season, the splendid balls and parties, the butterfly existence which seemed already so far away. All, in a sense, had been true—yet with the bitterness of party strife, the prolonged struggle for social reform, the violence of strikers and suffragettes, the threat of civil war in Ireland, and the growing menace of German military power, the pre-1914 period had had troubles enough of its own.

Note on Suffragettes
Women were eventually given the vote, first, at the age of thirty by an Act of 1918, and then in 1928 at the age of twenty-one.

7

Great Britain and the World

THE POSITION OF Great Britain as a world power and the growth of rivals and potential rivals had inevitably brought her into a closer and different contact with foreign nations. Before the Boer War the British thought of their country as standing securely alone, unentangled by alliances abroad, and protected by an invincible navy. This was the attitude often known as "splendid isolation". Splendid it might have been, but it had its dangers also. The Boer War had made them apparent: when this time of testing came Britain found herself without a friend in Europe.

Two Armed Camps in Europe

Europe itself was divided into two armed camps. On the one hand was the Triple Alliance of Germany, Austria-Hungary and Italy (dating from 1882); on the other was the Dual Alliance of France and Russia (dating from 1891). Britain stood outside the two camps, unattached to either. She had had her differences of opinion with Germany over colonial matters. But France was the traditional enemy, and there had been dangerous rivalry in Africa; Russia was feared as a threat to the Indian Empire, both across the North-West frontier, and as casting envious eyes on Constantinople, the eastern Mediterranean and the route to India. So long as one European group balanced the other, the political

117

existence of Britain might be secure. But if one group should defeat the other, what then?

The division of Europe into two groups was the result of certain basic European antagonisms. The oldest and most important was the rivalry between France and Germany, which since the defeat of France in the Franco-Prussian War of 1870 had taken the form of the quarrel over Alsace and Lorraine. These provinces had been taken from France by the Treaty of Frankfurt, which the French could never willingly accept any more than the Germans of a later age could willingly accept the Treaty of Versailles in 1919. Always between 1871 and 1914 there was in the minds of the French the idea of *Revanche*. Bismarck, in his time, knew this; and he built up the Triple Alliance to guarantee the security of Germany. So bad were relations between France and Germany, so many and so severe were the crises, that when one reads the detailed story of Franco-German relations during the years between 1870 and 1914, one feels that an armed clash between them was inevitable.

Another basic European antagonism was the clash of interest between Russia and Austria. These powers competed for control in south-east Europe. Russian imperialism had a possible field of expansion there, both in the decline of the Turkish Empire and as champion of the Slav peoples. Austria, on the other hand, felt herself the heir of an historic mission to carry Germanism south-eastwards against Slav and Turk alike. The decline of Turkey gave the opportunity— but Russia was a dangerous competitor, and when Russia stimulated national feeling among the Slav peoples she stirred up something inestimably dangerous to Austria. For the Empire of Austria-Hungary was not a German but a multi-racial empire, of Germans, Hungarians and Slavs, and Slav national feeling was something which would inevitably make for its break-up.

The British Attitude

Although England eventually established links with the Franco-Russian group, the move was for a long time by no means certain. There had, at other times, been other possibilities. There was, so far, no fundamental conflict of interest between Britain and Germany, and, while Bismarck was in power in Germany, the two countries had several times worked together. When, at the end of the nineteenth century, the Chinese Empire in decline offered a new field to Russian imperialism which endangered Britain's trade with China, Britain turned to Germany. Joseph Chamberlain made three overtures during 1898–1910 with the object of an alliance. Although, in the end nothing came of these overtures —there were recriminations over the respective behaviours of British troops in the Boer War and German troops in the Franco-Prussian War—they do show a British anxiety to find friends.

The gradual change of policy from isolation to finding allies appears very clearly in the difference of attitude between Lord Salisbury (who had previously been Foreign Secretary as well as Prime Minister) and his new Foreign Secretary in 1900, Lord Lansdowne. The Foreign Office had gone so far as to draw up a draft convention in 1901 to include Britain in the Triple Alliance system. Salisbury wrote a memorandum on this draft convention, and showed that he did not think our isolation dangerous. "Have we ever felt that danger practically?" he asked. He went back to Napoleonic times for an example: "If we had succumbed in the revolutionary war, our fall would not have been due to our isolation. We had many allies, but they would not have saved us if the French Emperor had been able to command the Channel." Lord Lansdowne, however, in a memorandum of his own, wrote:

> I fully admit the force of the Prime Minister's observation that this country has until now fared well in spite of its international isolation. I think, however, that we may push too far the argument that, because we have in the past survived in spite of our isolation, we need have no misgivings as to the effect of that isolation in the future.

Salisbury appears to have been opposed to Britain's making an alliance with any European power or group. He was attached to the old concept of the Concert of Europe; he tried to keep the great powers working together, and disliked their combination into groups. He preferred Britain to maintain a position of independence, and believed that so long as this country supported right and justice she would never find herself left entirely alone. From a position of independence, Britain could speak more easily to either side in any disagreement, and could maintain the balance. Lansdowne, on the other hand, was more impressed than Salisbury by the dangers of a general jealousy of Britain uniting her enemies against her. He turned for support, first to Japan—this with Salisbury's cordial agreement—and next—after his former chief's retirement—to France.

Alliance With Japan

Britain's alliance with Japan in 1902 broke the long tradition of British independence or isolation, but it was in reality an event unconnected with the great power groupings of Europe. It was the Far Eastern question which brought Britain into alliance with Japan, for Britain felt that the Japanese navy could play a useful part in maintaining the *status quo*. Japan, like Britain, disliked the expansion of Russia at the expense of China where Japan had her own interests involved. The treaty with Britain would enable Japan to deal with Russia without becoming involved also with Russia's ally, France, for the treaty guaranteed the *status quo* in the Far East, with the provision that either Britain or Japan would come to the aid of the other if it were to be at war with two powers in defence of the *status quo*. In 1904–5 the Russo-Japanese War resulted in the defeat of Russia and the further rise of Japan. It resulted also in a strengthening of the Anglo-Japanese alliance which was extended to cover intervention if a party to the alliance found itself at war with even one power in the Far Eastern area.

Entente *With France*

Meanwhile British relations with Germany were growing worse and relations with France better. Delcassé, the French Foreign Minister, had learnt the lesson of Fashoda; he had realised the strength of Britain and her trump card in her navy. He saw that an *entente* with Britain would be more profitable to France than continued colonial rivalry. Unlike many French ministers he held office continuously for a respectable period, from 1898 to 1905, and when Lansdowne began to look round for friends abroad Delcassé was ready. Another factor in the situation was the character of Edward VII. He had a flair for personal contacts, liked travelling abroad, and all his life showed a preference for France rather than Germany as well as feeling a certain animosity for his nephew, the Kaiser. When Edward paid his first visit (in May 1903) to Paris since he had become King, the public still harboured resentful memories of Fashoda and had the Boer War much in their minds. But the King left behind him a Paris captivated by his charm. A visit next year to London by the French President and Delcassé met with a cordial reception. German writers have since supposed that King Edward had a policy-making power such as continental autocrats could exercise, and there arose the story of his *Einkreisungspolitik*, the encirclement of Germany, which was thought to explain the King's frequent visits abroad. But, of course, the British constitution did not allow a policy-making initiative to the King: it was personally, not officially, that Edward VII exercised an influence in favour of France.

The Anglo-French agreements known as the *Entente Cordiale* were reached in April 1904, after hard bargaining, which had been going on since the previous autumn, between Lansdowne and Delcassé. More important than personalities was the advantage that agreement was seen to hold for each side. To England in her exposed position and faced with the growing power of Germany it seemed very desirable to settle outstanding colonial problems which might one day flare up into war; in particular, it seemed desirable to buy off the hostility of France over the British position in Egypt, for Lord Cromer's work there was made difficult by French opposition in the international commission of the debt upon which, in part, the governing of Egypt depended. To France an even greater advantage offered—that the *Entente* would not merely settle outstanding disputes with Britain, but range Britain with France in face of Germany. The main Anglo-French treaty covered disputes over Newfoundland, West Africa, Egypt, Morocco, Siam, Madagascar and the New

Hebrides. Most important of all was the agreement reached over Egypt and Morocco: what it amounted to was that France recognised Britain's special position in Egypt, Britain recognised France's in Morocco, and each promised the other support in case of any change of status in either of the two overseas territories. In other words, Britain might keep Egypt, France might take Morocco.

Britain, of course, regarded the new agreement with France as a pacific one. A Foreign Office memorandum three years later summed up the official view: "In England the wish for improved relations with France was primarily but a fresh manifestation of the general tendency of British governments to take advantage of every opportunity to approach more closely to the ideal condition of living in honourable peace with all other States." But for Germans it was not so easy to take this view; the British view could be regarded simply as naïve or even hypocritical. Germans felt that Britain had abandoned isolation at last, and taken sides in the European struggle.

Entente *with Russia*

A little more than three years later, in August 1907, Britain signed an Anglo-Russian Convention which, following the plan of the Anglo-French *Entente,* settled the main causes of friction between the two countries. France, of course, had used all her efforts to bring about a better relationship between Britain and Russia, and as Russia herself had been greatly helped by important French loans she was all the more ready to listen to the advice of her ally. Sir Edward Grey, Foreign Secretary in the Liberal government, proved ready to take the necessary steps to improve relations with Russia—though this was not easy, for very many Liberals hated the idea of an agreement with the autocratic Tsardom, especially as it was not long since Nicholas II had suppressed the Duma (the embryo Russian parliament) after the unsuccessful revolution of 1905–6. Britain and Russia agreed to settle their difference in Persia, Afghanistan and Tibet. In Persia Russia gained the lion's share with a large sphere of influence (the Tsar would probably have annexed it altogether had it not been for Great Britain and her fears as to Russian expansion in Asia); in Afghanistan, Russia agreed to leave the control of foreign policy to Britain; and, in Tibet, they agreed not to interfere and only to negotiate with her through China, which held a superiority over her. All these matters were of Anglo-Russian significance. What was of a wider significance was the fact of the new *Entente* itself—the Triple *Entente* could be regarded as a grouping standing over against the Triple Alliance.

Although the *Entente* with France and Russia was not an alliance, although Britain was not committed to going to war on behalf of one or the other, in the various international crises which marked the period Britain was drawn closer to France—perhaps in the circumstances, this was inevitable, and, if so, then the German view was not far from the truth in regarding the formation of the *Entente* as marking Britain's having taken sides with one group in Europe rather than the other. Early in the first Moroccan crisis of 1905–6 (see p. 128) the French appear to have thought they had an assurance of British support. The Foreign Office had given no formal assurance, but King Edward may have spoken too easily on his holiday return from Biarritz to London. Again, early in 1906, the French sought from the new Liberal government some assurance of British support in case of an attack by Germany. The French ambassador put the question to Grey, and asked also if Britain would agree to military conversations as to the form such support might take. Grey answered that he could not commit Great Britain in advance. It seemed reasonable, however, to make some preparation lest the eventuality should arise, and Grey, after consulting the Prime Minister, Campbell-Bannerman, and also Asquith and Haldane, agreed to the military talks. Staff talks began at once, and continued until 1914. They were kept secret, not only from the public, but also from the Cabinet as a whole. The staff talks did not commit Britain to war in defence of France, but clearly they did imply a considerable strengthening of the *Entente*. At the same time the British and French navies were beginning to depend upon each other. Ever since the formation of the *Entente* the Admiralty had felt able to move naval strength from the Mediter-

ranean to the North Sea and Atlantic. Naval consultations
resulted by 1912 in a definite division of responsibility between the two fleets, Britain covering the Channel and the
north, France the Mediterranean, although again it was put
in writing that this did not mean an undertaking to go to war.
During the final crisis of 1914 the British government went
so far, on August 2nd, as to guarantee the coast and shipping
traffic of northern France against German naval action.

The German Danger

The play of personalities, the lessons of experience, and the
existence of common interests had brought the Triple *Entente*
into existence. But there were in the character and sentiment
of the German people certain traits which made negotiation
with Britain difficult and any close relationship even more so.
There was something overbearing and aggressive which was
disagreeable to the British; the Wilhelmstrasse (the German
Foreign Office) bargained, demanded compensation (a word
which used to irritate Lord Salisbury), and held not far off
the threat of force. "The way in which German policy in-
variably opened fire at once with its biggest guns," a German
historian has said, "was extremely antipathetic to English
statesmen, who were more tranquil and tolerant in their diplomatic intercourse and very sensitive to threats." The German Chancellor, Bülow, expressed his opinion of the British
in a memorandum he had written in 1899: "British politicians
know little of the Continent. . . . They are naïve. . . . They
believe with difficulty that others have bad motives. They are
very calm, very easy-going, very optimistic." He affirmed that
"there is no doubt that feeling in England generally is far
less anti-German than German feeling is anti-British", and he
went on to say that certain English newspaper correspond-
ents were dangerous to Germany because they knew "how
sharp and deep is the German dislike of England". This dislike of the British was understandable, being stimulated as it
was both by jealousy and the innate British superiority not
only towards Germany in particular but towards other nations
in general.

There was in Germany a long-standing tradition of exaggerated patriotism and militarism. One of the most famous German professors, H. von Treitschke, who had become professor of history at Berlin in 1874, had taught that force was the all-important characteristic of the state, and that war was in the nature of things and peace was to be thought of as something sentimental and weak. He spoke of "the moral majesty of war, and described it as a "medicine for mankind diseased". Treitschke, like so many Germans, had been carried away by the success of Bismarck in uniting Germany and creating the German Empire by force of arms. He had come to glorify militarism, and to feel contempt for foreign countries; among them, especially, he felt a dislike for England. There were in Germany from the 1880s onwards various organisations, official and unofficial, created to push German aims and ideals; there were, for example, the Colonial League, the Navy League, and the Pan-German League, and they all had prominent people among their members and also support from industry. The Pan-German movement and the Navy League were described by Eyre Crowe of the British Foreign Office as being "inspired by bitter and often scurrilous hostility to Great Britain". Eyre Crowe's mother and wife were German, and he had close contact with German thought and feeling. Another British observer described the Pan-German League as "claiming all German-speaking peoples as of German birth and kin. It aspires to the ultimate inclusion of the German-speaking cantons of Switzerland, of the Baltic provinces of Russia, of parts of Belgium and Luxemburg, and most important of all, of Holland with her littoral and her colonies".

Eyre Crowe wrote a lengthy memorandum in 1907, which was marked "most valuable" by Grey and which summed up the situation. As he put it, the German argument was: "A healthy and powerful state like Germany, with its 60,000,000 inhabitants, must expand, it cannot stand still, it must have territories. . . . Necessity has no law. The world belongs to the strong".

German writers, too, were producing works of an extreme nationalistic character, with such titles as *Greater Germany —the Task of the Twentieth Century,* and *War and Peace with England?* Among them, in 1911, was General von

Bernhardi who, in his *Germany and the next War*, echoed Treitschke and the German philosophers in defending force and war, and stressed the need of German expansion in just the way that Eyre Crowe had described.

Strong, healthy and flourishing peoples increase in numbers . . . they require a constant expansion of their frontiers. They require new territories for the accommodation of their surplus population. Since almost every part of the globe is inhabited, new territory must as a rule be obtained at the cost of its possessors, i.e. by conquest which thus becomes a law of necessity.

Great Britain, he thought, barred Germany's way, and was therefore an enemy. Germany must be prepared to meet this danger in the future. War he described in a later book as "the highest expression of true civilisation" and as "fought in the interest of biological, social and moral progress". Facing Germany he saw the alternatives of "world power or downfall".

German Naval Rivalry

The Franco-German quarrel over Alsace and Lorraine and the rivalry in south-east Europe of Austria and Russia were, as we have seen, two basic causes of friction in Europe. A third, though more recent, cause of friction was the naval rivalry between Britain and Germany. Germany was a country of great, and still growing, industrial strength. She had taken over her industrial system from Britain, profited by our mistakes, and by 1900 had surpassed Britain as an industrial nation. Her steel output was increasing much faster than in Britain. Her prosperity and self-confidence were based upon discipline and hard work in all classes of society. Naval rivalry, therefore, not only increased Britain's suspicion of Germany but led also to her seeking her own self-protection in the development of the *Entente* relationship with France and Russia. The first German navy law passed through the Reichstag in 1898, behind it the popular propaganda of the Navy League, the ambition of Admiral Tirpitz, and the enthusiasm of the Kaiser. But though the alleged danger from England was used to win support for the cost of the warships, the German navy did not then represent a serious threat to Britain.

But a few years later the German navy came to represent a real threat. In 1906 Britain launched the *Dreadnought,* which was the first of a new type of battleship, which outclassed all existing ships in its fire-power and in the speed of its turbine engines. At first, of course, this gave Britain a long lead, for the German shipyards took about two years to produce a comparable design, and it took eight years before the Kiel Canal was widened to allow the new dreadnought-class ships to pass between the Baltic and the North Sea. But at the same time the dreadnought offered Germany an opportunity: the British Liberal government was not inclined to build many of the new ships, for each ship was vastly expensive, so that if Germany quickly built a small number of the new ships she could, now that the great number of older British ships were obsolete, threaten the balance of naval power. So Bülow introduced a new and ambitious naval programme in 1907, and resisted all proposals for a limitation of naval armaments both from Britain alone or at the Second Hague Conference.

By 1909 it appeared that Germany was indeed catching up in the race of dreadnoughts. It was this threat that roused in Britain the cry: "We want eight and we won't wait." But in the next two years we built eighteen ships to Germany's nine. Thus Britain was still well ahead. Germany had gained nothing—save the exacerbation of her relations with Britain. Bethmann-Hollweg, who had followed Bülow as Chancellor, said that Germany needed a navy for the "general purposes of her greatness". In fact, however, Germany, which had already the most powerful army in Europe, hardly needed a navy as well. Churchill described the British fleet as a necessity but the German fleet as a luxury.

Crises

Between the formation of the Anglo-French *Entente* in 1904 and the outbreak in 1914 of the First World War there took place a number of crises each of which threatened the peace of Europe. When we look back these crises appear as a series which led, step by step, to the outbreak of war. Any one of the crises *might* have precipitated a general war, but in fact only the crisis of 1914 *did* so, and yet that particular crisis *might* have been solved by diplomacy as the earlier ones had been. But while Europe was divided into two armed camps, and crisis followed crisis, it was likely, if not inevitable, that eventually there would be war.

The first of these crises was over Morocco in 1905. France was extending her influence there at the expense of the weak sultan, and Germany chose to interfere. The Kaiser broke his Mediterranean cruise in March to land at Tangier, and made a speech—certain to reach newspaper headlines everywhere—proclaiming that the Sultan of Morocco was a free and independent sovereign and that Germany had "great and growing interest in Morocco" which his visit indicated he was determined to safeguard. This brusque interruption by the Kaiser was a challenge to France and to the *Entente*. What was more Germany demanded an international conference on Morocco and demanded the removal of Delcassé (the maker of the *Entente*) as a troublemaker. The French government were alarmed by German threats; it realised French unreadiness for war together with that of its ally Russia, made helpless by the Japanese war and by revolutionary outbreaks at home. The French government, therefore, gave way on both points, and the Conference of Algeciras met in January 1906. But at the conference Britain, Russia and Spain (and also the United States, now emerging on the European scene) backed France's claims. Thus, though Germany postponed the complete taking over of Morocco by France, in effect France's special interests there were recognised by everyone, and this was not at all what Germany had intended.

In 1908 there was a crisis in south-eastern Europe. A revolution in Turkey made it possible for Austria to annex outright the territory of Bosnia-Herzegovina which she had been allowed to occupy since the Congress of Berlin in 1878. The Austrian action in itself might not be surprising. But the inhabitants of these Turkish provinces were Slavs, a population of 1,500,000, and Serbia had been dreaming of their joining in a Slav state. The Serbs urged Russia to resist by arms the loss of the Bosnian Slavs to Austria, and the armies of Serbia and Montenegro were on a war footing during the winter of 1908–9. But when Russia (with little support from France, and Grey taking an independent line) gave way on this, Serbia perforce had to do so also—a great disappointment to the Serbs and a heavy diplomatic defeat for Russia. However—and in this lay a grave danger to European peace in the future—the Serbs could see that Russia, if she valued her prestige and leadership of the Slav peoples, could not afford to disappoint the Serbs a second time.

Meanwhile fresh trouble was brewing in Morocco. France was extending her powers in Morocco, and Germany was unwilling to concede French claims. When in 1911 France sent a force to Fez, the Moroccan capital, to maintain order, Germany sent the gunboat *Panther* to Agadir avowedly for the protection of German lives and interests. This brusque show of force by Germany alarmed France, and also led Britain to fear that Germany might intend to establish a west-Atlantic German base, of much more direct concern to Britain than the internal affairs of Morocco. Heavy pressure was put on France by Germany. Lloyd George (after consulting Asquith and Grey) used a speech he was due to make at the Mansion House in London to give a public warning to Germany. The warning was effective; the Germans, although enraged, disclaimed interest in the Moroccan coast. But the war scare continued—some mobilisation preparations were set on foot in Germany and France, and also in Britain and Belgium. Russia, however, was not more eager to fight for French claims now than France had been over the Russian interest in Bosnia in 1908, and Austria also was uninterested. The result was a compromise: Germany finally abandoned Morocco to France (Morocco became a French protectorate), and France ceded territory in the Congo to Germany in compensation.

Although the Agadir crisis was settled, it meant that it would be more difficult, perhaps impossible, to settle another crisis on the same scale by peaceful means. The blow to Russia's prestige in 1908 now had its counterpart in the failure of the *Panther's* spring. Neither country would find it easy to give way a second time. Once more, too, in Germany Britain was blamed for her support of France. Lloyd George's speech was called "a menace, a challenge, a humiliating challenge". The Germans, however, had not despaired of breaking up the Franco-British relationship. In 1912 Haldane was invited to Berlin to see if some limitation could be arrived at of the naval competition between the two countries and of its great expense. In return Britain might, it was thought, agree to a declaration of British neutrality "if war was forced upon Germany". But Britain was unwilling to make any agreement which might weaken the *Entente*, and the German proposal came to nothing.

Next, two wars in the Balkans caused further alarms. A Balkan League was formed against Turkey, and in the campaigns of 1912–13 the Serbs, Bulgars, Greeks and Montenegrins in co-operation all but flung the Turks out of Europe altogether. But the victories of the Balkan League naturally affected the interests, fears and jealousies of the great powers. In particular, Austria was determined to prevent Serbia from maintaining ports on the Adriatic, for her victories had given her a temporary access to the sea. About this time, however, the great powers agreed, as also on leaving Constantinople and its environs to the Turks—a settlement along these lines was made by the Treaty of London on May 30th, 1913. Then a second Balkan war broke out when the victors quarrelled over the spoils, and Bulgaria attacked Serbia. The Serbs routed the Bulgars, and Greeks and Rumanians also attacked Bulgaria. But Austria by diplomatic pressure saved Bulgaria from complete destruction, and in October 1913, compelled the Serbs to evacuate Albania, a new state which the great powers had created in order to keep the Serbs from the sea. Serbia thus remained a land-locked state, with a sense of grievance, although she and also Greece and tiny Montenegro had nearly doubled their area in each case as a result of their victories in the Balkan wars. Another result of the Balkan wars was that Turkey came to look more than ever to Germany and Austria for support against the Slavs, and a German general was sent to Turkey to reorganise the army. The Kaiser saw his opportunity. As he put it: "It is now a question of getting hold of every gun which is ready in the Balkans to go off for Austria against the Slavs, therefore a Turco-Bulgarian alliance with Austria is certainly to be accepted." Bulgaria was likely to side with the Triple Alliance for the sake of revenge on Serbia. Most clear of all was the position of Serbia: she stood out, after the victorious campaigns, as the champion of the south Slavs. Against her, Austria looked round for the moment to wage what she could regard as a preventive war.

Britain and the War Danger

All this might seem remote enough from Britain. Yet all the great continental powers were making military preparations, in expectation of a short war in which effective transport, well-planned mobilisation measures, and the element of surprise might prove decisive, and in a general war Britain might become involved or see the balance of power seriously upset. Britain, certainly, of all the powers, was least concerned with the clash of interests in the Balkans, and had herself no interest in undertaking any war in Europe. The dancers at the London hotels and the thousands outside St. Paul's as New Year's Eve passed into New Year's Day, 1914, had no idea that England was entering a fateful year. Lloyd George, who had spent Christmas surrounded by his family at Criccieth, saw it as the most favourable moment in twenty years for reduction in armaments. "Our relations with Germany," he said, "are infinitely more friendly now than they have been for years. The strain is completely relaxed. Both countries seem to have realised that they have nothing to gain, and everything to lose, by a quarrel." Grey had striven steadily for peace through international understanding. An American [1] historian has said of him:

> There was one man who had a vision of a new order—Sir Edward Grey. . . . Although he steadily strengthened the Triple Entente as a bulwark against possible German aggression—that was only one side of his policy. He was so far from pursuing a policy of encirclement that he told the Russian Ambassador in London that the isolation of Germany

[1] B. E. Schmitt: *The Coming of the War.*

would be the surest road to war; for that reason he accepted the Triple Alliance and made no attempt, however covert, to weaken it. In his mind, the *entente* with France was not to be used against Germany policy or German interests. What he desired and worked for was an understanding with Germany, on the condition, as he phrased it, that it "must not put us back into the bad old relation with France and Russia". If this could be achieved, the way would be open to the creation of an effective Concert of Europe.

Serajevo and the Coming of War

But the way was not to be opened. An event, remote and apparently unconnected with British interests and policy, was the occasion for the outbreak of the Great War or the First World War, as it is generally known nowadays. On June 28th, 1914, the Archduke Franz Ferdinand was assassinated in Serajevo, the Bosnian capital. The Archduke was Austrian heir-apparent, but Bosnia was now Austrian territory and the assassins, therefore, though Bosnian Serbs by race, were Austrian subjects. But they had come recently from Belgrade with arms, and Austria supposed that this murder could at least indirectly be connected with the Serbian government; Austria saw in it a heaven-sent opportunity to punish Serbia and curtail her pan-Slav activities which were so dangerous to the multi-racial Austrian Empire. First Austria got a promise of full support from Germany. Then she sent an ultimatum to Serbia on July 23rd—she had waited until a state visit of the French President and Prime Minister to St Petersburg was over lest they might take the opportunity to plan with Russia a counter-stroke. In vain did Serbia accept most of the demands, with only forty-eight hours allowed to her to decide. On July 28th Austria declared war (next day the Austrians bombarded Belgrade).

There was, however, still hope of localising the conflict. Germany now suggested moderation to Austria; the Kaiser had swung around a little, for the Serbs had acted with unexpected submissiveness, and the British had shown signs of taking a serious line when the fleet was not dispersed on July 26th at the end of the naval manoeuvres. Britain also advised settlement of the dispute by mediation of the four powers not directly concerned. But on July 30th came general mobilisation in Russia—Russia remembering the Bosnian crisis of 1908–9 felt that she could not fail Serbia a second time. France, after making an effort to get Russia to avoid open mobilisation, mobilised her own forces in accordance with her military agreement with Russia. The French mobilisation was only just ahead of the German. Germany declared war on Russia on August 1st. France was pledged to follow Russia, but actually Germany declared war on France on August 3rd.

Britain's part was still uncertain. The Triple *Entente* was an understanding, not an alliance; there was no automatic obligation on Britain to go to war. Germany tried to gain British neutrality, by an offer to take no French territory in Europe, but this was refused. Grey meanwhile was pressing for a conference of the great powers. What Grey was not in a position to do was to warn Germany that Britain would intervene if the conflict became general. The British public and parliament itself did not at first see any reason for Britain to be drawn in. The man in the street asked why he should be involved on account of "a lot of Serbian murderers". Almost to the end, nation and cabinet were divided; Burns and Morley resigned. The turning point came with the German invasion of Belgium. Belgian neutrality was guaranteed by a treaty of 1839, and Britain was one of the guarantors. By August 3rd it was known that the Germans had demanded, and Belgium had refused, the passage of the German armies through Belgium. It was the German threat to Belgium which gave Grey the support he needed in parliament and the country. On August 4th German troops invaded Belgium, and a British demand was sent to Germany for assurance that Belgian neutrality would be respected.

When the time-limit ran out at 11 p.m. (midnight in Berlin), Britain was at war.

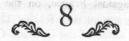

8

The First World War

AT DAWN ON August 22nd, 1914, a British patrol fired the first British shot in the First World War; it was the first British shot to be fired in Western Europe since Waterloo in 1815. The British Expeditionary Force of about 100,000 men under Sir John French, had crossed the Channel in safety, smoothly and efficiently, and taken up its position on Belgian territory and to the left of the French armies, according to the plans made in the Anglo-French staff talks. But already bitter and bloody struggles had taken place in France and Belgium.

German Invasion of Belgium and France

The Germans began the war in the west by the invasion of Belgium, their troops passing through the Belgian capital to make a wide sweep southwards into France. This was their famous Schlieffen Plan—named after Count Schlieffen, former chief-of-staff, who had worked out in 1905 a means of dealing with the threat of two-front war which the Franco-Russian Dual Alliance involved. The problem was how to knock out France, before the huge but slow-moving Russian armies could come into action. The plan consisted of a vast encircling movement: the German armies of the right wing pivoting upon Lorraine as the centre of the whole German chain of armies would wheel through Belgium, move southwards to take or by-pass Paris, and then drive the retreating

French armies eastwards into a trap between their pursuers and the German centre in Lorraine. In putting this plan into operation, Germany kept a comparatively small force on the Russian frontier; against France, on the other hand, there were seven armies amounting to 1½ million men.

The French, too, had their plan—to take the initiative and attack. They would attack the German centre—Lorraine, and Alsace—and break the German chain of armies in two. Their plan was based on the idea that "a great part of the German forces will be concentrated on the common frontier". This idea misled the French generals; they neglected the possibility of a German advance in strength through Belgium. And, as it was, the French plan failed. The French attacks—frontal assaults on positions defended by machineguns—incurred record casualties, of some 300,000 men; and they failed to penetrate the lost provinces or to hold up the main German advance through Belgium. The Belgian resistance was brave, and the forts around Liège did hold up the Germans for some days, but by August 22nd the German forces were well to the south of Brussels, and coming into contact with British patrols.

The British Expeditionary Force was in position at Mons, in Belgium, on the extreme left of the line of French armies facing the Germans. Sunday morning, August 23rd, was still quiet; the church bells rang, the people of the nearby villages dressed in their Sunday-best were setting out for church, trains were bringing holiday-makers into Mons. But the Germans were approaching steadily from the north, and the patrol encounters gave way to battle. All day it went on: the Germans advanced in mass formations, and were mown down by British rifle fire. But German numbers were overwhelming, their artillery fire on Mons itself was deadly, and the French army on the right was in retreat. During the night the British forces with difficulty extricated themselves, and the long retreat from Mons began. The Germans were checked for a moment at Le Cateau by General Smith-Dorrien (a splendid soldier who had been at Isandhlwana, and Omdurman, and through the Boer War), but the retreat continued—for thirteen days. By the end of August the Germans were threatening Paris, and the French government moved to Bordeaux. By September 5th the German First, Second and Third Armies had crossed the Marne. The British were now actually south-east of Paris. But the Germans had over-reached themselves. General Joffre, the French commander-in-chief, with great courage and skill, moved the French and British forces into a counter-attack. The Battle of the Marne, from September 6th to 10th, was one of the decisive battles of history in that it saved the French armies from the intended encirclement: the Germans were forced back, Paris was saved, and there was even talk of the war being over by Christmas. The Germans, however, established themselves, some forty miles back, along the Aisne. Stalemate—but the Schlieffen Plan had failed.

To the north there was still territory unoccupied by either side, and there was a kind of race for the Channel ports. The British force was transferred to the north, and, with the remnant of the Belgian army, fought the First Battle of Ypres (October 21st—November 11th). The Ypres salient, just inside the Belgian frontier, saw some of the fiercest fighting and became the grave of many, or most, of the Expeditionary Force (50,000 casualties). But the salient was held, and the British established a line due north and south from the Channel coast to the River Somme. The trenches became during the winter a permanent line stretching from the sea to the Swiss frontier.

Meanwhile stalemate had been reached on the Eastern Front also. Russian Poland provided Russia with a great salient from which she could strike north and south. To the north she invaded East Prussia, but the Germans sent two great generals, Hindenburg and Ludendorff, against the Russians, whose armies were destroyed in late August and mid-September at Tannenberg and the Masurian Lakes. East Prussia was secure. But in the south the Russians were successful; they over-ran the Austrian province of Galicia and began to threaten the German industrial area of Silesia. German counter-attacks in the north, however, towards Warsaw, relieved the Russian pressure. Against Serbia, too, the Austrians had had but little success; twice they invaded the country only to be driven out.

From the very beginning of the war, Britain's naval supremacy had been quietly effective. It was the navy which, ensured the safe transport of the Expeditionary Force to France, and also guaranteed this country against invasion while the greater part of its army was abroad. It also cut off Germany from her colonies overseas; our ally, Japan, was free to conquer German positions in the Far East and the North Pacific, and British and Dominion forces were able to conquer the German colonies in Africa. The British navy swept all German commerce from the seas, and also destroyed the few German cruisers which were at sea when war broke out. The *Emden* did much harm to British shipping, until she was destroyed by the Australian navy. A small German squadron sank two British warships at Coronel (off the coast of Chile), but soon afterwards was destroyed by a stronger British force off the Falkland Islands. Most important of all was the British naval blockade. Not only was the English Channel tightly closed to Germany, but also the passage between Scotland and Norway. It is true that the United States claimed the rights of neutral commerce with belligerents, and we were forced to allow neutral ships to carry some goods through the blockade if we could not prove they were contraband of war. But the blockade did have a considerable effect in making things difficult for Germany.

The Western Front: Trench Warfare

The stalemate on the Western Front was, in fact, a prolonged and bloody struggle; it went on for the four years' duration of the war. Each spring or summer both the Allies and the Germans planned a break-through. Huge numbers of men and vast quantities of munitions were involved on either side. Britain had to build up and train great armies as the continental powers had already done. Asquith had, immediately on the outbreak of war, appointed Kitchener as War Secretary. He was a national figure, and he realised, as so many people did not, that the war could be a long one. His task was to build the new, volunteer armies. He called, in the first month, for 500,000 volunteers. Two and a half million volunteers came in during the first eighteen months of the war. "Your country needs you" was his call. Kitchener's picture on the recruiting posters, Lloyd George commented, had more effect than all the appeals of the political leaders. But more still was needed, and in 1916 the government introduced conscription, which marked a break in an old British tradition and brought the resignation of one minister, the Home Secretary, Sir John Simon.

Men and munitions against men and munitions—that was the picture of war. The continuous lines of trenches did not allow free manoeuvre. Surprise attack was difficult, for the trench systems were elaborate and well defended, and they had to be heavily bombarded by artillery before the infantry could attack. Observation balloons and scouting planes also kept the opposing side under observation. Ma-

chine guns were deadly to infantry when they did advance, and shell holes and mud presented them with special difficulties when the land had been torn up by shell fire. Casualties among the attackers were almost always far heavier than among the defenders. Advances made were small, and the advantage remained generally with the defenders.

How to break this stalemate? That was the question. Then —and since—that question has given rise to controversy. There were, briefly, two views of what should be done. One, held by the military leaders, British and French, was that attack and break-through should be on the Western Front; the other view, represented by two dynamic personalities, Lloyd George and Churchill, was that some way must be found of attacking elsewhere, in south-eastern Europe, by, for example, a knock-out blow to Turkey (which had joined the Central Powers in October 1914, and barred Allied communications with Russia) or by an invasion of the Balkans to attack Austria. There were powerful arguments on both sides. The easterners could point to past wars won by wide turning movements, and in France there were no exposed flanks to turn—hence the need to look elsewhere. But the westerners pointed out that the enemy held the interior lines and could thus move his forces quickly from one front to the other. They also had on their side the maxim that you cannot be too strong at the decisive point. A break-through on the west would be decisive. A victory over the Turks would not compensate for a German capture of Amiens. Therefore, at all costs, the west must be held. Hence the building up of men and materials in the west; hence the prolonged trench warfare, the great offensives, and the heavy slaughter.

Thus it was that war on the Western Front was a series of great bombardments and attacks. In 1915 the Germans tried to break through the Ypres Salient, and in this Second Battle of Ypres (April) they used poison gas but even so did not break the British defence. The British lost heavily in attacks at Neuve Chapelle (in February), Festubert (May), and Loos (September). The gains were small, and shortly after Loos French was replaced as commander-in-chief by Sir Douglas

Haig. Meanwhile in Champagne the French were launching attacks in a serious but vain attempt to relieve the German pressure on the Russian forces on the Eastern Front.

In 1916 the Germans launched a terrific onslaught on Verdun which brought six months of fighting. The French resisted with the utmost tenacity, and their casualties, in this case, outweighed those of the attackers. *On ne passera pas* was their proud slogan—and they held Verdun. Verdun became a symbol of what French courage could do. To relieve France, Britain now put on a major offensive, backed by the new volunteer armies and a vast supply of shells. The Battle of the Somme lasted from July to November. The flower of British manhood perished, but week after week the attack was renewed. Haig has been severely criticised for this—and later—offensives, but the Germans suffered heavily also. During the winter they quietly withdrew their main forces some miles to prepared positions known as the Hindenburg line.

In 1917 a French attack at the Chemin des Dames failed so terribly that a mutiny broke out in the French Army. It was suppressed, but British efforts to relieve the French brought the bloody offensive of the Third Battle of Ypres, or Passchendaele, a four-month battle in the mud of a wet autumn. The Battle of Cambrai in November saw the first large-scale use of a British invention—tanks; some had been tried on the Somme, but Cambrai saw a much larger number in action. The Germans were taken by surprise, and the British made, for the time, an advance.

The War on Other Fronts: The Dardanelles, 1915

The great struggles in the west have so far mostly occupied our attention, but there were other fronts and other dangers. In 1915 Italy joined the Allies as the result of promises of Austrian and other territory made in the secret Treaty of London (April 26th, 1915) which induced her to abandon the Triple Alliance; Italy's intervention pinned down a considerable Austrian force in the defence of the Alpine frontier. There were British campaigns against Turkey, and also campaigns in the Balkans and on the Russian Front.

A first British objective in the campaign against Turkey was to establish communication with Russia by way of the Dardanelles, and so help Russia by sending her munitions. In March 1915, the navy bombarded the Dardanelles forts and tried to force a way through the Straits, but several ships were sunk or disabled by mines, and the attack was called off. The attack, however, gave the Turks warning of dangers to come, and they strengthened their fortifications. When British forces were landed in April on six beaches they could do little more than establish themselves along the shore; they could not dislodge the Turks from the hills. A further landing followed in August at Suvla Bay. But again in spite of great heroism the troops could not establish themselves on the heights commanding the sea. The British and Anzacs (Australian and New Zealand Army Corps) were at a deadlock. After great anxiety and hesitation, Kitchener decided on evacuation, which took place in December 1915 and the early days of January 1916; the evacuation, almost by a miracle, was carried out without loss. Another campaign against Turkey was fought by a force based on India; it made its way through Mesopotamia towards Baghdad, but was brought to a halt and besieged in Kut, where eventually it had to surrender in April 1916. The British troops, now prisoners of the Turks, suffered terribly on the long, forced march to the interior of Turkey.

In the Balkans the Allied cause suffered disaster. Bulgaria joined the Central Powers; Bulgaria attacked Serbia from the east, and Germany and Austria sent a strong army across the Danube which overwhelmed Serbia completely in November 1915. In the next summer, Rumania also, which had joined the Allies, was over-run by the Germans. The Russians, though they could not save the Balkans, made great efforts in 1915 and 1916. They could not stop the German advance of 1915 which led to the fall of Warsaw, the German occupation of Russian Poland, and the capture of a million Russians. But the Russian armies showed great powers of endurance and of revival; in the winter of 1915–16 they won a number of victories over the Turks in the Caucasus, and in June 1916, they broke through the main Austrian line to threaten Budapest. The Germans saved the situation by attacking from the north, but Austria was shaken—before the end of the year the Austrian government was putting out peace feelers.

Political Changes at Home:
Lloyd George Takes the Place of Asquith

It is not altogether surprising that the terrible strain of indecisive battles and the daily crushing casualty lists produced political tensions at home. Criticism of the government developed—particularly over shortages of shells and the Dardanelles controversy—and in May 1915, Asquith gave way to Conservative pressure and constructed a new, Coalition government to contain the Conservative leaders. As a result of these changes Lloyd George was made head of a new Ministry of Munitions, where his drive and administrative powers brought about a great improvement—from now on the army was well supplied with shells and guns.

Early in the next year the Coalition had to face the grave peril of new and serious trouble in Ireland. In spite of the fact that Home Rule had become law in 1914—though suspended for the period of the war—and that thousands of Irishmen had enlisted and were fighting with the British forces, the old hatred had revived in Ireland. The Sinn Feiners ("Ourselves Alone") aimed at establishing an Irish Republic, and to do so they sought to use the opportunity offered by the war and opened negotiations with Germany. Arms were to be sent in a cargo ship and a submarine. The ship was sunk, but the submarine landed Sir Roger Casement, who had come from Germany to lead the rebellion. However, he was captured (and subsequently executed). The plotters tried to call the rising off, but it was too late. The Irish Rebellion broke out in Easter Week, 1916, and led to five days of bitter fighting in Dublin, especially around the Post Office in which the so-called Provisional Government of the Irish Republic had been set up. When the rising had been suppressed, the leaders were court-martialled and shot. The rebellion had failed, but it left a new legacy of hatred and disorder.

During 1916 there were also other important events at

home. The summer was marked by the loss of Kitchener. He was on his way to Russia to see if we could help them with their shortage of munitions, when the cruiser *Hampshire* struck a mine of the Orkneys and sank with most of its crew. His place as War Secretary was taken by Lloyd George, who, had it not been for a change of arrangements because of the Irish Rebellion, would have accompanied Kitchener on his ill-fated mission.

Meanwhile impatience was growing with Asquith's conduct of the war. Conservative members of the government were particularly critical. It was felt that Asquith, though he had the wisdom and judgment to be an outstanding premier in time of peace, had not the drive and quickness of decision which war demanded. And there was a man to hand who had these qualities—Lloyd George. It was Lloyd George who suggested to Asquith that there might be a special War Cabinet with some minister other than the premier in charge. To run the war was a full-time job, Lloyd George argued, but Asquith should remain head of the ordinary Cabinet. The compromise suggestion was not acceptable, and Lloyd George resigned from the government. His resignation brought its break-up, and the resignation of Asquith himself. Thereupon, the King called upon Lloyd George to become Prime Minister, and he formed a new government (in December 1916) composed of Conservatives and some Liberals. Most of the Liberal ministers, however, sided with Asquith, and relinquished office; among them was Grey, who was followed at the Foreign Office by Balfour. This was the beginning of the great split in the Liberal Party, between those who followed Asquith and those who supported Lloyd George, and it was a split which led to the decline of the Liberal Party and later greatly aided the rise of Labour. But most of this was in the future. To run the war Lloyd George set up a small War Cabinet with himself as chairman. It proved to be effective, and it and the drive and optimism of the new Prime Minister helped much to win the war.

The War at Sea

While the prolonged struggles were waged on land, there

was a relentless war at sea also. The one great naval battle of
the war was fought off Jutland (north Denmark) on May
31st, 1916. Advance squadrons of the British (Admiral Beatty's battle cruisers) and German fleets engaged, and the British
suffered heavily, two of the battle cruisers being sunk by
German salvoes. Behind Beatty was the main British fleet
under Jellicoe, and the German fleet moved up behind its
own advanced force. But as the two fleets made contact, Jellicoe showed extreme caution in being unwilling to risk his
ships against the dangers of mines and torpedoes. After some
manoeuvering and confused fighting, the German fleet was
able to withdraw and to escape. The Germans inflicted
heavier loss than they suffered; but though they had skilfully
escaped from the numerically superior British force, they did
not venture to come out and fight again. The British, however, were also increasingly unwilling to risk the fleet in
distant waters—for both sides the submarine was a growing
menace to the big ship.

The British blockade of Germany was maintained throughout, and the Germans found various ways of hitting back
at Britain. The raids by great airships, the Zeppelins, caused
loss of life, and there were also raids by small aeroplanes,
but neither airships nor planes were a real military danger.
What was a real menace to Britain was Germany's submarine campaign. Just as Britain maintained a naval blockade of Germany so the German submarines attempted to
blockade the coasts of Britain. Early in 1915 German
submarines started to attack Allied and neutral ships (though
it was against international law to sink them unless due warning had been given). This aroused indignation in America,
especially when, in February, a hundred Americans were lost
among the 1,198 persons drowned when a submarine sank the
large British liner, the *Lusitania*. The outrage might have provoked America into war, but President Wilson was not yet
convinced of the necessity to abandon his country's traditional
neutrality. American protests did, however, make Germany
forbid attacks on neutrals, and, since it was difficult for a
submarine to identify shipping, this meant the effect of the
German blockade was very much diminished.

In 1917 the Germans made a desperate attempt with their

submarines to force Britain into surrender. The Germans
thought that, even if their action did bring America into the
war, they could starve Britain into submission before the
American intervention could make any difference to the
fighting. Germany had built a fleet of about 300 submarines,
and on February 1st, 1917, she commenced a policy of un-
restricted submarine warfare—any ship, Allied or neutral,
trying to sail to or from Britain would be sunk at sight. The
first four months of 1917 were marked by a heavy increase
in shipping losses: the outlook was serious indeed, for the
country was reduced to a corn supply of six weeks and,
though people did not know it, it was thought in government circles that November would mark the limit of endurance. But Britain found methods of dealing with the
submarine menace. The new Prime Minister, Lloyd George,
was responsible for the most important of them. He suggested
that convoys should be tried. The Admiralty had maintained
that a convoy system was impracticable because of the difficulty of avoiding collision among groups of ships in dark-
ness, and that the naval vessels could not protect bunched
merchant ships against attack by submarine. But Lloyd
George proved to be right. The convoy system was tried, and
turned out to be a great success: by the end of the war the
navy had convoyed 88,000 vessels with a loss of only 436.
Other measures were the mining of the German coasts, the
Dover Straits, and the North Sea between the Orkneys and
Norway; the use of "Q" ships (armed vessels looking out-
wardly like merchant ships) to draw on and then sink the
enemy submarines; and the rationing of food in Britain. By
the end of 1917 the danger was over.

America Comes In

The German submarine campaign brought America into
the war. In March 1917, five American ships were sunk, and
in April America declared war. What had begun as a European struggle was now a world war. The Germans had been
right in thinking that it would be some time before American
troops could be brought over to fight on the Western Front.
But the American navy was able at once to help in protect-

ing ships crossing the Atlantic, and there were no more complaints about the British blockade, the effects of which on Germany were thus intensified. The American intervention had also its effect upon morale: the Allies looked forward to new and increasing numbers of men and quantities of material, and the Germans were correspondingly depressed.

The Russian Revolution

The year 1917 which saw America come to the aid of the Allied Powers was marked also by the loss of Russia, for during those months were taking place the events known collectively as the Russian Revolution, events which, though but dimly understood at the time in the West, were to change fundamentally not only the lot of Russia and its place in the Allied war effort, but also the future development of Europe and the world. Of all the Great Powers, Russia was the most backward, the least developed industrially, the least well prepared to fight a prolonged war, and the one whose government was most autocratic, most out of touch with the people, and most corrupt and ineffective. The great defeats, the heavy losses in casualties and prisoners, and the sufferings of the deprived civilian population made Russia ready for desperate measures of reform—most of all for measures which would end the terrible war. After a bad winter, with starving people waiting in queues for food, riots broke out in the streets of Petrograd (now Leningrad) in March. The Tsar's government was no longer strong enough—with the loss of its best troops in the war and the general lack of support for it—to suppress revolution. On March 15th the Tsar was forced to abdicate, and a Provisional Government was set up. This first revolution was of the kind familiar enough in Europe—a change of government by force, the setting up of a constitutional government in place of an autocratic one. This revolution was welcomed in Britain and France; it was thought that the new government would be democratic, that it would clean up corruption in Russia, and that it would carry on the war more effectively. And indeed Kerensky, who came to head the Provisional Government, did try hard to carry on the war. But, after initial successes in a summer offensive against the Austrians, the Russian army began to break up. Discipline was failing—there was no will strong enough to impose order and direction once the central government had lost its former power.

For now a formidable rival had taken shape to destroy the Provisional Government. This new force was that of Communism, or Bolshevism, as it was often called in Russia. The Germans had taken every advantage of the situation; they had allowed Lenin and other Communist leaders to travel through Germany from exile in order to enter Russia, and they had moved their troops forward sufficiently to threaten Petrograd. Lenin had studied Karl Marx; he was full of the idea of the class war and the workers' revolution. Lenin realised that now he had the opportunity to launch such a revolution; he used the Soviets (or councils) of Workers and Soldiers; these councils undermined discipline in the army and also the obedience of people to the government. In November the second revolution, Lenin's revolution, took place. In Petrograd the Communists rushed the Winter Palace and overthrew the Provisional Government (Kerensky managed to escape), and seized the public buildings and railway stations. The Communist Revolution succeeded; Lenin was successful not only in seizing power, but in consolidating it also. And this meant for the Allies the end of Russia's war effort, for Lenin was determined to make peace as soon as possible. An armistice was signed in December, and in March 1918, the Russians accepted peace at any price—the Treaty of Brest-Litovsk was signed, the terms of which were most severe for Russia.

The Russian Revolution and the American entry into the war, were, of course, the outstanding events of 1917. But there were a number of moves on subsidiary fronts. On what might be described as the outer edge of the war, the British achieved some considerable successes against Turkey. The campaign in Mesopotamia was resumed: Kut was reoccupied in February, Baghdad was taken in the next month, and the rest of the territory was gradually brought under control. Other British forces based on the Suez Canal (which the Turks had attacked in vain) advanced in October into Palestine. General Allenby commanded the advancing army, while Lawrence and his Arabs carried on harassing tactics in the desert against the Turks. Pushing the Turkish forces back before him, Allenby succeeded just before Christmas in entering Jerusalem, the Holy City which no Christian army had entered since the time of the Crusades. In October 1917, there was sudden activity on the Italian front; the Germans sent help to the Austrians, and this reinforced army inflicted a disaster on the Italians at Caporetto. The Austro-German forces broke through the Italian lines and very nearly took Venice. British and French reinforcements had to be sent, and the advance was at last stemmed. It was not until October of the following year that Italy was sufficiently recovered to take the offensive, and to win the victory of <u>Vittorio Veneto</u> shortly before the Austrian Empire broke up. ↑ Italian victory

The Final German Effort, March 1918

In 1918 the Germans had their last opportunity of victory. They were secure in the east, now that Russia was out of the war. This, therefore, was the moment to strike a knock-out blow on the Western Front before the new American armies were trained and could be brought across the Atlantic to France. The Germans delivered a series of great attacks, dramatic in their intensity, and threatening at this eleventh hour to break through the Allied defence in France. In March, with a superiority of almost three to one, the Germans attacked the British line from Arras southwards to the River Oise. In a week the Germans won back the area of the old Somme battlefield which the British had won at such heavy cost in 1916. They advanced to within ten miles of Amiens, and only just failed to smash through the junction point of the British and French armies. At this desperate time, the Allies at last agreed to set up an Allied supreme command: the French commander-in-chief, Foch, was given supreme authority over all the Allied forces in the field. The Americans were urged to send over troops as soon as possible.

In April, the Germans made a second attack, just south of Ypres. It looked as if Ypres might fall at last, opening the way for the Germans to the Channel ports. A German break-through at Ypres would have cut off part of our armies to the north, and disrupted the supply of all our forces through the ports. The British fought, said Haig's Order of the Day, "with their backs to the wall". Then came a third great attack, at the end of May, against the French lines in Champagne. Here, too, the Germans made a considerable advance, reaching once again the River Marne. The French were sorely pressed, and they only just managed to hold their ground along the Marne.

But the Germans were exhausted by this supreme effort, and they had not the necessary reserves to follow up their first attacks. When they attacked again in July and crossed the Marne, Foch was able to hold them and launch a counter-attack which was virtually a second Battle of the Marne. The Allies now had on their side the advantage of a supreme command, the use of tanks on an increased scale, and the American armies growing at the rate of 250,000 men landed in France every month. It was Foch's policy to follow offensive by offensive at different points on the Allied line in order to give the Germans no rest and no time to recover.

Allied Counter-Attack

On August 8th the British launched a big attack at Villers-Bretonneux in front of Amiens. The "black day of the German army" broke the nerve of Ludendorff who had been the main military driving force on the German side. The British army advanced over the old Somme battlefield again, and on towards the Hindenburg Line. The Americans won their first independent victory by straightening out the St Mihiel salient near Verdun, the French and Americans both advanced towards the frontier, and the Belgians also attacked from Ypres. When, at the end of September, the British penetrated the Hindenburg Line, Ludendorff, who knew that both Germany and her allies were breaking up, advised his government that it should seek peace. It took another six weeks to negotiate an armistice.

The last months of the war saw important developments on the subsidiary fronts. The first of the countries on the German side to be knocked out of the war was Bulgaria. Already, in late 1915, the Allies had established a base at Salonika on Greek territory, made possible by disunity in Greece between factions supporting, on the one hand Germany, on the other, the Allies. Now in September 1918, a French general advanced with a composite force (French, British, Serb and Greek) against Bulgaria, routed her army, and brought about her surrender. The surrender of Bulgaria meant the isolation of Turkey—threatened also by British advances from Jerusalem into Syria, where Damascus was taken on October 1st, and in northern Mesopotamia towards Mosul. Turkey now made an armistice, the Dardanelles were at last opened, and Allied troops entered Constantinople. The Italian victory of Vittorio Veneto (won by joint Italian and British forces) drove the Austrians out of Italy, and in November revolution broke out in Vienna.

The End of the War

In Germany itself things were going from bad to worse for the Germans. The British blockade had had its effect on the civilian population; the navy was restive after having been in port so long, and mutiny broke out; and on November 9th the Kaiser abdicated and fled to Holland. The armistice was signed, in a railway coach, on November 11th. Germany was defeated—the British were back where our war had started, at Mons, the French were approaching Lorraine, and the Americans had reached Sedan.

The war was over. The long and dreadful slaughter which filled the years of 1914 to 1918 with horror and mourning had ceased. Wild rejoicing broke out in the victorious countries; people could breathe again and look with hope to the future. But in reality there was little ground for hope or optimism. The losses had been on a scale unknown before—both victorious and defeated nations had suffered enormous casualties, eight million men killed and twenty million wounded. The fighting had shown how thin was the veneer of our boasted Western civilisation, and how soon mankind could fall back into savagery. Savagery, too, had armed itself with new scientific weapons of mass slaughter.

War itself had changed, or was changing, towards total

conflict. Civilians had been involved as well as soldiers. Each combatant nation had found its resources engaged to an extent unknown before. Britain felt this in particular. In the past her chief weapon had been sea power; in the previous continental wars, the British part, over and above the war at sea, had been to subsidise her continental allies and send small professional armies to assist them. But during the First World War Britain had to use her naval power more intensely than ever before, had also to organise her industrial and financial system to meet her own and her Allies needs for munitions, and had in addition to send huge armies to fight overseas. Britain had survived, indeed had triumphed, but Europe and the world had been fundamentally shaken and could never be the same again. Four ancient dynasties were overthrown—the Hohenzollerns in Germany, the Habsburgs in Austria, the Romanoffs in Russia, and, soon after the war, the Ottomans in Turkey. Impoverishment, unemployment and economic difficulties were soon to face governments with new and ever more difficult problems. And away in the east, in Russia, although with its cells everywhere where poverty or suffering offered a hold, Communism offered a new challenge to the whole existing order.

9

Peace—the Unfulfilled Promise

WHEN THE WAR ended there was a widespread hope
that the long agony might prove to be the way to a
better world, and the idealism of President Wilson of the
United States, General Smuts of South Africa, and Lord Cecil
in this country produced the League of Nations with its noble
object of preventing war in future. But at the same time so
prolonged a struggle as the First World War with its heavy
casualty-lists could not but leave behind it a legacy of bitterness and even a desire for revenge. During the election of
December 1918, cabinet ministers spoke of hanging the Kaiser
and of getting out of Germany everything "you can squeeze
out of a lemon and a bit more". Lloyd George himself declared: "We propose to demand the whole cost of the war".
In addition to resentment against foreign enemies, old tides
of economic criticism and social change were gathering
new force. After so great a catastrophe which had come
about under the older social auspices, the voices of Labour
and the trade unions were more likely to be heeded. During
the election Lloyd George spoke of making Britain a "fit
country for heroes to live in". But together with the problems
of demobilisation, decontrol of industry, and the revival
of normal civilian life, any government would be faced with
tasks which would test its capacity to the full.

Lloyd George Coalition Victory

First came the general election—the last had been in 1910,

and parliament had prolonged its own life during the war. Lloyd George fought the election as leader of the Coalition, for his wartime Conservative allies continued to back him. His action widened and perpetuated the split in the Liberal Party, and all but destroyed it. The Coalition won an overwhelming victory. The independent Liberals were reduced to 26; Asquith lost his seat. The Labour Party (which had withdrawn from the Coalition immediately after the war finished) lost its leaders, Ramsay MacDonald and Philip Snowden, but increased its popular vote and its members in parliament from 42 to 59 which allowed it to claim to be the official Opposition. Already, too, during the election, the Labour Party was attacked as the representative of Bolshevism; Lloyd George denounced Labour as "being run by the extreme pacifist, Bolshevist group". Lloyd George, the Leader of the Coalition government, "the man who won the war", dominated the political scene.

New Troubles and New Problems

Though peace had come, and with it a hope of better things, new troubles followed hot-foot on the end of the war. During the winter the great influenza epidemic, spreading from Europe to England, increased in severity; 150,000 persons died in England and Wales. Resentment at slow demobilisation led to demonstrations and riots in some army camps. The new year, 1919, opened with the menace of a general strike, which might have been the precursor of revolution (for the Russian example was much in people's minds). There was serious trouble in Glasgow in January and February—the principal factories were closed by the strikers, the red flag was hoisted, and great demonstrations took place in the streets. But the government took resolute action: troops were brought up around the city, and, after fighting between the police and the crowds, were marched through the streets. But in Glasgow, and elsewhere, the immediate danger passed. For during 1919 there was a short-lived boom: a wave of speculative company promotion and expansion encouraged business people and gave temporary employment to workers.

During the war, under the pressure of national need, there had been a great growth in government control. Railways and mines were controlled, and many factories were set up by the Ministry of Munitions. Towards the end of the war there was idealistic thinking about what could be done afterwards to better the people's lot. A Ministry of Reconstruction was created in 1917, and from its efforts came a flow of reports on social and economic matters. The Labour Party had its own schemes for nationalisation. But nothing came of all this. Business men demanded decontrol of industry, and the government allowed wartime controls to come to an end, and sold its war surplus goods and many of the national factories. On the other hand, in some spheres, there was a marked movement towards amalgamation and large-scale organisation. In banking, the Big Five emerged, from a consolidation of the ownership of numerous smaller private banks. Government control of railways and mines ended in 1921, but the Railways Act of that year formed the 120 companies into four systems—the Great Western, the L.M.S., the L.N.E.R., and the Southern. The strongest demand for nationalisation came—with the threat of a national strike—from the Miners' Federation early in 1919. Lloyd George played for time by the appointment of the Sankey Commission (under Sir John Sankey, later to be Lord Chancellor). But by the time it reported in the summer public interest had declined, and the Peace Conference in Paris was occupying attention. In any case the Sankey Commission produced not one, but several, conflicting reports, which enabled the government to escape the necessity of taking action.

Another experiment the government tried was the holding in February 1919, of a National Industrial Conference of trade unionists and employers. The conference led to proposals for public works (roads, light railways, afforestation, housing, etc.) to be undertaken and pushed forward to relieve unemployment in bad times—an idea of which much was to be heard in the future, though little came of it at the time and the standing conference which had been created came to an end in the summer of 1921.

The danger of strikes—to press demands for better conditions and higher wages—continued through 1919, 1920 and

1921: there was a police strike in 1919, a nation-wide railway strike later in the year, and a miners' strike in 1920, after which the government passed the Emergency Powers Act to safeguard essential services endangered by a strike, and another miners' strike in 1921, which almost led to a general strike, only averted on what workers called "Black Friday" when the railwaymen and transport workers abandoned the miners. But at the same time the government was doing something to help the poor by its Housing Act of 1919 and the Unemployment Insurance Act of 1920. Local Authorities were given subsidies to undertake the provision of houses at low rents (there was a considerable housing shortage, because ordinary building had stopped during the war), and Lloyd George's unemployment insurance of 1911 was greatly expanded to bring in almost all wage-earners, except those in agriculture and domestic service.

The Peace Settlement and the League of Nations

Most important, however, among the events of 1919, was the Peace Conference which opened in Paris on January 18th. The peace settlement which was made there was intended for all time, but in fact lasted for only twenty years. More ambitious and comprehensive, for it was a world settlement, it was less successful than the Congress of Vienna which did leave a Europe which would for a hundred years escape a general war. To Paris came the representatives of the Allied and Associated Powers, from every continent. But among them the main decisions were necessarily made by the Big Four—President Wilson of the U.S.A., Clemenceau, Prime Minister of France, Lloyd George, and Orlando of Italy, though, Italy being comparatively weak, the Big Four was in reality a Big Three. Each of them had his faults, but it has been said that "each was better than the prevailing majority of the public he served." Clemenceau, "the Tiger", was considered by many Frenchmen to be too moderate in his attitude to Germany. Lloyd George on the whole wanted a just peace and a new Europe; he urged moderation towards Germany, lest severity should strengthen Bolshevism and throw Germany into the arms of Russia. But he was held by his followers to the election pledges he had made in the excitement of victory. When he wished to reduce the reparations to be paid by Germany, 370 M.P.s sent him a telegram to remind him of his promise that Germany must pay. It was, in any case, impossible to make a peace settlement that would satisfy everyone, yet settlement of some kind there must be—for Europe was falling into chaos, with the break-down of the Austrian Empire and the independence of Czechs, Hungarians, Poles and Slavs, Communist régimes in Hungary and in Bavaria, and widespread hunger and the spectre of Communism in central Europe generally.

The Treaty of Versailles, signed with Germany on June 28th, 1919, was the most important of the peace treaties. It was signed in the same *Galerie des Glaces* of the Louis XIV Palace where the German Empire had been proclaimed in 1871. Just as Bismarck's new German Empire had emerged with the defeat of France in the Franco-Prussian War, so the defeat of Germany in the First World War gave to France a marked though shortlived pre-eminence in Europe. Representatives of Germany did not take part in the making of the treaty (though they were permitted to submit observations in writing when it had been drafted), and this allowed the Germans to claim later on that the treaty was a *Diktat*. Nevertheless, when all things are considered, the treaty was not unreasonable: it did not destroy Germany, it made a real attempt to solve problems of nationality, and it did much to secure France by providing for the disarmament of Germany (and indeed, as the future turned out, there was no general war in Europe *until* Germany was once more rearmed).

The territorial settlement may be quickly summarised, the changes being largely justified on the basis of nationality. Alsace and Lorraine were returned to France, the territory of West Prussia and Posen went to the Poles, thus creating the "Polish Corridor" to give the new state of Poland access to the sea. North Schleswig went to Denmark, and three small border districts to Belgium. Danzig, a German port dominating Polish access to the sea, was made a Free City, and, in the west, the Saar area was placed under international control for fifteen years (for its sovereignty was disputed between France and Germany) while its coal mines were given to France as compensation for war losses. Upper Silesia, a mining area in the south-east of Germany, proved a great difficulty; it was at first allotted to Poland, but after a plebiscite (on the insistence of Lloyd George) in which the Germans gained a majority in the proportion of 14:9, it was partitioned between Poland and Germany. Overseas, too, Germany lost all her colonies. In spite of these losses, the German homeland was in no way dismembered, but remained a unity and a potentially powerful country in the heart of Europe. The 1930s were to show how quickly she could rearm and become again a menace, threatening all her neighbours with political domination or conquest.

This, indeed, was what the French feared, but events were to show how powerless were France and her allies to prevent it. But by the Treaty of Versailles they tried hard to deprive Germany of the means for war. The German army was reduced to a force of 100,000 (volunteers enlisted for twelve years to prevent the building up of large reserves), and Germany was to have no air force, no large warships, no heavy artillery—her existing equipment, including the navy, had been handed over under the armistice terms. As a further safeguard against possible aggression in the future, German territory on the left bank of the Rhine was demilitarised together with a further strip on the right bank, and the Rhineland was put under an Allied military occupation. Thus a wide, important and populous *undefended* area was established along the French frontier: the Germans had fought two wars on French Territory in the past, but it seemed in 1919 that, if there was to be a third war, it would be fought on German soil.

The disarmament of Germany was highly reasonable. And it did not seem unreasonable to ask Germany to make some financial reparation for the cost of the war—after all victorious Germany had compelled France to pay the cost of the war of 1870. But to pay the whole cost of the world war was impossible for any nation (except perhaps the U.S.A.). No sum was fixed by the treaty, but later the Allies demanded £11,000,000,000, subsequently reduced to £6,600,-000,000. Germany could not pay in gold, and suggestions to pay in services or in goods met opposition. If German

labour were put to do repair work in France, it would interfere with employment for French workers; if German coal
were sent in payment, it would compete with the product of
French and British mines. Attempts to make Germany pay
led to occupation of the Ruhr in 1923 by French and Belgian
troops, which in turn left behind a new legacy of hatred.
The Germans also bitterly denounced the war guilt clause—
which justified reparations by placing the whole responsibility for the outbreak of war upon Germany and her allies.
The reparations provisions are certainly the part of the
Versailles Treaty which is most open to criticism.

Treaties were signed also with the other enemy powers. In
the years to come the Treaty of Versailles was often blamed
for all the shortcomings of the peace settlement. But it had
nothing to do with the break-up of the Austrian Empire—
this was happening in any case at the end of the war, and
was confirmed in the other treaties. Austria and Hungary had
fallen apart amid the disasters which fell upon them at the
end of the war. The Czech provinces of Moravia and Bo-
hemia also broke away, and formed the basis of the new
state of Czechoslovakia. Other territories, previously Austrian
or Hungarian, were joined with Serbia to make another new
state, Yugoslavia. Austria lost also Galicia to the new Poland, and the South Tyrol to Italy. These changes, though
justifiable on grounds of nationality, caused many new problems. The settlement with Turkey involved, perhaps, the
greatest difficulty of all. The Treaty of Sèvres, in 1920, had
set up what was virtually an Allied tutelage over what was
left of the old Ottoman Empire. Allied forces took possession
of the Straits and controlled Constantinople and the Sultan's
government, while Greek troops were landed on the west
coast of Asia Minor to occupy Smyrna and its hinterland to
establish an age-old claim to lands where Greek colonists
had settled since the days of Ancient Greece. But meanwhile the Turkish general, Mustafa Kemal, who had repulsed
the Allies at the Dardanelles, formed a new, nationalist government at Ankara in the heart of Asia Minor, and, after a
terrific struggle, drove out the Greeks in 1922. The Ottoman
Sultan fled, and Kemal remained as head of the new Turkey,
declared in the following year to be a republic. A settlement

was made with the Allies by the Treaty of Lausanne in 1923. The treaty marked a signal victory for the Turks. The defeat of the Greeks had signified the downfall of Allied policy, particularly that of Lloyd George who had backed the Greeks. For a moment British troops in Turkey had faced the victorious Turkish nationalists at Chanak, and war was narrowly averted. The failure of his Turkish policy contributed to the decline of Lloyd George's Coalition government.

In spite of all this, the peace settlement (Versailles and the other treaties taken collectively) had established the liberal idea of self-determination on a basis of nationality—more Europeans than ever before were now under governments which they willingly accepted; they had, too, some direct control over these governments for they were democratic in form and subject to popular election. The greatest triumph of liberal idealism, however, was to be seen in the creation of the League of Nations. It was for this, above all, that President Wilson had striven; it was due to his personal efforts that the League Covenant (the clauses setting up and defining the new League) was written into each of the peace treaties as an integral part of it. It was understood, also, from the outset that eventually ex-enemy states would be admitted to membership of the League. The League was provided with appropriate institutions: an Assembly, a kind of parliament of the world to which all members would send representatives; a Council, with the Great Powers automatically members, which could take action to prevent war; and, a secretariat, or international civil service. Other tasks were also to be undertaken. The former enemy colonies were placed under mandate to certain powers which were to govern them as "a sacred trust of civilisation". There was to be an International Labour Organisation, and machinery was created for the better arrangement of other matters, such as world health. But most important, of course, were the provisions for redress of international grievances, for enquiry and arbitration in case of international disputes, and for sanctions in case of aggression. All this established a new ideal in international relations—world peace and its maintenance by collective security. What happened in the outcome, the history of the next few years will reveal.

Events Leading to the Irish Free State

While new standards of international behaviour were being established with the creation of the League of Nations, Britain and Ireland were moving into the final and bitterest stage of their age-old controversy. The problems of Irish home rule and of Ulster re-emerged, for, after the suppression of the wartime Easter rising of 1916, the influence of the extremist Sinn Fein party grew rapidly, under men like Arthur Griffith, De Valera and Michael Collins. In the election of 1918 Sinn Fein swept the board in Ireland; outside of Ulster they won every seat except four. The newly elected M.P's refused to come to Westminster, but met in Dublin instead as a self-constituted Irish parliament. In January 1919, they declared Irish independence and the establishment of the Irish Republic which had been proclaimed at the Easter rising. What was more they carried their Irish grievances overseas —to the Peace Conference in Paris, though little came of this, and to America, where a visit by De Valera publicised their cause and stirred the embers of bitter American-Irish hatred. From America five million dollars came in to the Irish cause. At home the Irish leaders built up an armed force, the I.R.A. (Irish Republican Army), and gradually this led to guerilla warfare between the Irish and the British government, still officially the government of Ireland, backed by British troops and by the Royal Irish Constabulary. The R.I.C. was reinforced by men from England, recruited from among ex-soldiers, and became notorious as the Black and Tans (since there were insufficient R.I.C. uniforms available, they were dressed in surplus khaki uniforms and black belts). On both sides there were acts of barbarism, and the savagery and reprisals cast a dark shadow over the years 1919–22.

Viewed in its historic setting, the scene was, indeed, a strange one: Lloyd George, the Liberal, the one-time supporter of Home Rule for Ireland, was now head of a government which was struggling fiercely to suppress resistance in Ireland. At the same time, it may be agreed that the Irish were extremely difficult to deal with, and not only their resistance to British forces but also their subsequent disagreements among themselves and unwillingness to accept compromise show clearly enough that it was not easy to reach a settlement.

So the war—for war it was—was fought out, but without trenches, battle fronts, and, on the Irish side, without uniforms. Normal life went on, but in Dublin and Cork and in south-west Ireland generally there were ambushes, night attacks, kidnappings, murders in the streets, bomb explosions, and reprisals by the Black and Tans, and sometimes these actions developed into miniature battles. Sometimes, too, houses and public buildings were set on fire and destroyed.

By the Government of Ireland Act of December 1920, the British government took a step forward. Ireland was to have home rule, and the Act provided for two Irish parliaments, one for Ulster and one for the south. But the Sinn Fein leaders would have nothing to do with this. Ulster, however, accepted, and her own parliament and government were set up. Thus Ireland was partitioned; this much, at least, was settled. And the British government could concentrate on Sinn Fein: either to force it into submission, or to bring it to terms.

Meanwhile the struggle went on. During the winter martial law was declared in southern Ireland—no Irish jury would convict a prisoner accused of the murder of a policeman or soldier. At the same time public opinion in England was growing against the government's policy of repression. The Labour Party condemned it. The Liberal newspapers were against it; Asquith denounced the policy of reprisals early in 1921. Some of the Conservatives were coming round to a similar view. Rumours of a truce grew; some peace feelers were put out by each side. In July a truce was agreed on, and in October Irish representatives, led by Arthur Griffith and Michael Collins, came to London for a conference. The conference was a success. Agreement was reached on December 6th, 1921: an Irish Free State was set up (excluding Ulster) with its own parliament; Ireland in fact secured the status of a Dominion, remaining in the Empire. The Irish leaders had, indeed, made great concessions and showed real statesmanship in realising what was possible.

But the agreement was only narrowly ratified by the Irish parliament, and the Sinn Fein party was split: some for, some against, the treaty with England. De Valera was against. The split led now to a civil war in Ireland, which cost Michael Collins his life in an ambush. But eventually the new Irish government established order—it executed 77 rebels in six months compared with 24 by the British during 1920–21. Ireland was free; and in the following years took steps to reduce her ties with England. DeValera came into power in 1932, and in 1937 declared Ireland "a sovereign independent democratic state".

End of the Coalition: Lloyd George in the Wilderness

In October 1922, there came a decisive change in British politics: the fall of the Coalition. Its position had been weakened by the failure of Lloyd George's Turkish policy, by the indignation at government policy in Ireland, and by economic depression and unemployment. But the Coalition was not brought low by popular dislike, and there was nothing to show that it was particularly unpopular. Its fall was the result of action by the Conservative Party. Although its leaders were ministers under Lloyd George, many of its lesser men and rank-and-file were beginning to fear for the future of the party. There had been talk of a fusion of Conservatives and L. G. Liberals, of a new political grouping. Out-and-out Conservatives reflected that Lloyd George had broken the Liberal Party, and feared he might break the Conservative Party also. This was the argument of a new man, Stanley Baldwin, at the Conservative Party meeting at the Carlton Club on October 19th. Bonar Law spoke also in favour of Conservative independence. The meeting voted in favour of leaving the Coalition. Lloyd George thereupon resigned as premier, and the King called upon Bonar Law who formed a Conservative government. In the election of November it secured a majority of 88 over Liberals and Labour put together. Everyone thought Lloyd George would come back again one day, but he never did; a period of political weakness had begun, and there were no more big men until disaster in war brought Churchill into power in 1940.

Baldwin, and Ramsey MacDonald's First Labour Government

Baldwin followed Bonar Law (who resigned because of ill health) as premier in May 1923. He had built up a reputation as a man of sound common sense, simple, honest, and of good will. But though he had feared that Lloyd George might smash the Conservative Party, Baldwin's own first move was to lose it the election at the end of 1923. For, in the face of unemployment, Baldwin turned to a policy of protection. This united the Liberals: Asquith and Lloyd George joined together to fight for free trade, and 158 Liberals were elected. Labour had 191 candidates elected. Together Labour and Liberals outnumbered the Conservatives. Asquith decided that the Liberals should support Labour, and so the first Labour government in our history was formed under Ramsay MacDonald. But Labour was in office, not power, for they could do nothing without Liberal votes. However, no socialist legislation was forthcoming. In less than a year Labour was defeated over a proposal to come to a trade agreement with Bolshevik Russia. During the election at the end of 1924 fear of Communism produced a strong reaction, and gave the Conservatives under Baldwin a secure majority.

The General Strike

During Baldwin's second government (1924–9) economic depression continued, and industrial unrest came to a head. One cause of industrial trouble was, perhaps, the action of Winston Churchill, who had now joined the Conservatives and become Chancellor of the Exchequer. Churchill in 1925 restored the gold standard, by giving the pound sterling its pre-war value in terms of gold, in an attempt to re-establish Britain's old financial position when the City of London was the world's financial centre. Raising the value of the pound was good for bankers and importers who would get more for their pounds, but bad for exporters, for foreign buyers would have to pay more to get pounds to pay for British goods. Thus the export trade suffered, and employers wished to reduce wages in order to reduce prices. But the workers saw this as a threat to their whole standard of life.

The immediate cause of trouble was the wages of the miners. The coal owners maintained that coal prices must be lowered to sell in foreign markets, and that to do this wages must be reduced. The miners refused, and were supported by the other trade unions. The General Council of the Trades Union Congress organised a General Strike in 1926, and this time there was no holding back, no "Black Friday". Everywhere factories stopped, transport came to a halt and newspapers did not appear. This was a threat not to employers only, but to the country as a whole. Many people felt that a General Strike was more than a strike; it was a blow at the constitution. The government put into operation carefully prepared measures to provide supplies and essential services, making use of private motorists and volunteer drivers for trams, buses and lorries, under police and military protection where necessary. Fortunately, however, the strike leaders were not willing to carry the strike through at the cost of revolution. Behind the scenes there were negotiations; Baldwin broadcast, promising justice both to miners and owners. On the ninth day the T.U.C. called off the strike, and life returned to normal (though the miners nevertheless continued their strike, and could not avoid reductions in their wages). The General Strike was a most remarkable event; it proved to the unions how far they could go, and that they could not succeed by direct action. There was no further move of this kind. At the same time the outcome of the strike showed how little real bitterness there was between class and class, for what might have been the beginning of revolution passed off almost peacefully.

Unemployment

But the times were hard. The years between the wars are still remembered as the years of prolonged unemployment, which was a heavy burden to the nation. The taxpayer was drained to provide the dole, workers who should have been producing were standing idle, and to be without work for a long period and dependent on the dole brought hardship, discouragement and hopelessness to the unemployed themselves. Unemployment was partly due to a weakening of Britain's economic position relative to other countries. During the war Britain had had to sell a large part of her overseas investments; after the war Britain was still burdened with vast debts to the United States on account of war supplies purchased for herself and her allies. Still more serious was the decline in British exports, for Britain was losing the position of economic leadership she had held in the nineteenth century. Foreign countries built their own industries, and put up tariffs against British goods; foreign countries, putting up new factories, installed the latest machinery, while Britain, already industrialised a long time, might be using obsolete machinery and old-fashioned methods. Coal mining suffered severely, when Germany, France and Poland got their mines going again after recovering from the effects of the war. Iron, steel and shipping suffered, for these industries had grown greatly in America, Japan and Germany. Japanese competition hit the British textile industry, for Japanese workmen were paid low wages and Jap products were consequently cheap. All this caused unemployment in Britain.

The Second Labour Government, the World Slump and the National Government

At the General Election of 1929 Lloyd George led the Liberal Party with a carefully thought-out plan—backed by the famous economist, J.M., later Lord, Keynes—"We can conquer unemployment". The plan was for the government to put into operation a great scheme of public works. The Liberals, although they gained ground, did not win, and the opportunity for a bold effort at national reconstruction was lost. The Labour Party was victor, and a second Labour government under Ramsay MacDonald was set up, although again dependent upon Liberal votes in parliament. But the Labour government was very unlucky: it was caught in a world slump, which made unemployment not only a British but a world problem. In October 1929 a sudden and disastrous panic seized Wall Street—the New York Stock Exchange— and this led to a great economic slump in the United States which, like a chain reaction, spread to the rest of the world.

It was the worst slump in history: world trade declined catastrophically, and unemployment mounted in the years following 1929. At its worst, there were three million unemployed in Britain, six million in Germany, and twelve million in the United States. And economic slump brought political repercussions: the Labour Party was destroyed, temporarily, in 1931; in Germany, Hitler came to power in 1933.

The Labour Party in office found itself unable to deal with the growing unemployment which followed the world slump, and it also found that the country's financial system was threatened by the growing cost of the dole. The May Committee—a Committee on National Expenditure appointed by the government, and under the chairmanship of Sir George May—reported in the middle of 1931 that the rising cost of unemployment relief was unbalancing the budget, and that drastic cuts must be made to avoid national bankruptcy. The result was a financial crisis: foreigners withdrew deposits from the Bank of England, and to save itself the Bank had to ask for credits from France and America. The government prepared to make economies (consultations were held with Liberal and Conservative opposition leaders), but could not get agreement among its members to a ten per cent. cut in the dole. MacDonald thereupon brought his government to an end, but he decided with Conservative and Liberal support to stay on himself as Prime Minister. He formed a new coalition or National government; it consisted of some of his personal supporters from the Labour Party, some Liberals (but not Lloyd George who was seriously ill at the time), and the rest Conservatives, and his policy had the backing of the Conservative Party generally. Under the new government the cuts in expenditure were made, and in the election which followed the National coalition beat the Labour opposition by ten to one. Next year, amid the misgivings of the Liberals, a protective tariff was introduced; whether in spite of or because of this, the economic situation gradually returned to something more normal. MacDonald retired in 1935, and soon afterwards he died; the National government continued under Baldwin, and later, under Neville Chamberlain.

In 1936 there was a constitutional crisis which Baldwin

handled skilfully. King George V died in January, and was followed as King by the popular Prince of Wales who became Edward VIII. In the autumn it was learned that he was in love with an American lady, who had already divorced two husbands. Neither British nor Dominion governments considered her suitable to become Queen. Rather than give way, Edward abdicated and married Mrs Simpson. His brother became King as George VI—the third King in one year.

Hitler and the Events Leading to the Second World War

The world slump and the disastrous effect of unemployment helped Hitler into power in Germany, and this in turn was the cause of events which led directly to the Second World War. The history of the years between the two World Wars falls, from the international point of view, into three phases: first, the making of the world peace settlement by the Peace Conference in Paris; second, the building up of the new international order of the League of Nations to take the place of the so-called "international anarchy" of the pre-war years; third, the decline of the new international order as the fascist dictators rose to power and challenged the international ideal with military force. From 1919 onwards, until at least the mid–1930s, men's hopes were centered on the League of Nations. People in Britain who were young at the end of the war of 1914–18 grew up to take it for granted that it had really been "the war to end war". War seemed to belong to the past, to the Dark Ages. In the future, it was thought, the League of Nations would solve international disputes with justice and without recourse to war. A new era of peace, disarmament and social progress would follow what already seemed an old-fashioned past of ignorance, folly, barbarism and war. But the rise of the fascist dictators brought a rude awakening: even in America, where people were most prosperous, most secure, and most optimistic, the Wall Street crash and its results were a severe shock, and events in Europe and elsewhere forced them in a few years to contemplate again a world at war.

The League of Nations had represented the triumph of

liberalism in international affairs. The Paris peace settlement, with its treaties based on national self-determination, was a triumph for the liberal ideal in national affairs also—it was assumed that democratic government would become in time the accepted form of government everywhere. But, in reality, the world was not ready for this. As early as 1922 Mussolini established a dictatorship in Italy—the result of disappointed war hopes, economic difficulties, and upper and middle class fear of Communism. Communist violence on the left produced violent reaction on the right—for Fascism was a movement of extreme nationalism prepared to return blow for blow with the exponents of the Moscow brand of internationalism. But the emergence of violent and ruthless national dictatorship meant the end of Italian democracy and, although this was not realised for some years, a real threat to the League of Nations which was inherently democratic. In the 1920s in Spain and Portugal also dictatorships replaced weak parliamentary régimes; in Poland and also in the Baltic states and in the Balkans, during the 1920s and 1930s there was dictatorship or a tendency towards it, and democracy at best worked uneasily in new surroundings. A serious threat to peace came also in the Far East in 1931: Japan attacked Manchuria, an outlying Chinese territory, and conquered it—in face of world opinion and of the report of the League of Nations commission sent out to investigate. No further action, however, was taken by the League.

But the greatest blow to democracy and the new order of things came in Germany when, in January 1933, Hitler became chancellor and set up his Nazi (National Socialist) régime, a fascist dictatorship of the most extreme form. Germany had in the years before 1929 showed signs of settling down; economic conditions improved somewhat, and parliamentary government was working. But the Germans did not forget the Treaty of Versailles and the humiliation of defeat; the nation had a proud military tradition, strengthened by Bismarck's victories over Denmark, Austria and France which had made possible the founding of the German Empire, and the Germans had been trained to obedience, and would therefore be inclined to follow easily an outstanding leader. The world slump brought to Germany new disasters, financial crisis in 1931 and mounting unemployment. In desperation, they turned to Hitler, a man of magnetic power, who could arouse the passion and enthusiasm of the masses. His Nazi Party rose to dominance as unemployment increased during the years of the slump; in 1928 there were only 13 Nazis in the German parliament, but in 1932 there were 230, and the Nazis were the largest single party. In this situation, it was inevitable that, sooner or later, the Nazis must form a government. Once installed, Hitler carried through his revolution: he dissolved the other parties and the trade unions, and made the Nazi Party supreme.

Hitler's objects were to regain all the lost territories inhabited or partly inhabited by Germans, and then to go on to the conquest of vast areas of Russia to make a future homeland for a vastly expanded German race. To do this he must first rearm. By rearmament, by building munition factories, ships and planes and by building new strategic roads, he could solve the unemployment problem. Of course, at first, he dare not reveal all this. He moved cautiously, talking of peace and even of disarmament, throwing dust in the eyes of England and France. Numerous famous people—including the Duke and Duchess of Windsor (i.e., the former Edward VIII and his wife, the former Mrs Simpson) and even Lloyd George—went to Germany to visit Hitler. And so weak were the governments of England and France and other countries that they were deceived, or if not completely deceived, were too fearful and divided among themselves to take any strong action in time to stop Hitler. Only a few bold and farsighted men—prominent among whom were Churchill, Anthony Eden, and Duff Cooper—warned the country against the growing danger, and their warnings went unheeded. Events appeared to move relentlessly in favour of the dictators.

In 1935 Italy, in order to add to her colonial empire, attacked Abyssinia—both were members of the League. The League condemned Italy, but no effective action was taken, and Mussolini conquered Abyssinia. Italy and Germany in November 1936 joined in the Rome–Berlin Axis. Hitler had observed that both Japan and Italy had "got away with it". And he knew that what Mussolini's Italy could do, Hitler's new Germany could do far better. By 1936 German rearmament was progressing fast, and Hitler risked the reoccupation of the demilitarised Rhineland. In 1938 he seized Austria. Then the pressure was put on Czechoslovakia—ostensibly to bring to Germany the German-speaking frontier area, the Sudetenland. Neville Chamberlain put off war for a year by going three times to Germany to meet Hitler—and giving him all he asked at Munich. Early in 1939 Germany over-ran all Czechoslovakia. Now even Chamberlain could see that Hitler could not be trusted, and was out for the domination of Europe. Poland's turn came next: the Nazi pressure of propaganda, abuse and threat was applied. To make Britain's position clear Chamberlain guaranteed Poland Britain's help in case of German aggression. But Hitler made a pact with Soviet Russia to allow him a free hand, and on September 1st, 1939, Germany attacked Poland. On September 3rd Britain and France entered the war in support of Poland. The Second World War had begun.

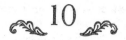

10

The Second World War

Hitler's War: The Attack on Poland

THE SECOND WORLD WAR was, above all, Hitler's war. It was caused by the simple fact that Hitler was armed, ready and determined ruthlessly to assert the interests of Germany at the expense of other nations which stood in its way. Either those other nations must give in, or they must resist by force. September 1939 was the moment at which resistance by force began. But for a long time everything went in Hitler's favour. The new Nazi army launched its first blow, its first *Blitzkrieg* or lightning war, at Poland. The *Luftwaffe* (air force) knocked out the small Polish air bases, broke up communications, and pinned the Polish land forces to the ground they held. Meanwhile German armies advanced from north and south, from north-west and south-west; whole Polish units were surrounded and destroyed by the German tanks. The Poles fought with desperate courage— the British and French could give no help, and dared not risk reprisals by starting a war in the air over Germany— and soon Warsaw was encircled. Then, on September 17th, the Russians invaded from the east. After a heroic resistance to the Germans, Warsaw surrendered on September 27th. Poland was divided, under the terms of their pact, between Germany and Russia.

The "Phoney" War

On the west, throughout the winter, everything remained

171

quiet. This was the period of the "phoney war" or *Sitzkrieg* (sitting war). School children were evacuated from London, but the expected bombing did not come. The British Expeditionary Force crossed the Channel, and took up its position along the Franco-Belgian frontier, under the French Supreme Command. The Maginot and Siegfried Lines, the fortified defences which had been built before the war along the frontiers of France and Germany, appeared to have brought stalemate. Hitler's ally, Italy, remained neutral for the time being. In the west rumours were rife, and bewilderment was general. The Germans had gained their immediate objective. Hitler waited to see if England or France would back out of the war; the Germans could afford to wait for a time, and meanwhile the bewildered Allies sent planes over Germany to drop, not bombs, but leaflets which urged the Germans to rise against Hitler.

At sea, however, war was real enough. Once more, as in 1914, the British navy applied a blockade against Germany. Using mine-laying, naval patrol and aircraft, the navy cut off overseas supplies to Germany, by preventing the passage of the Dover Straits and barring the way across the North Sea between Scotland and Norway. From the very start the German U-boats were a menace: on September 3rd, the liner *Athenia* was sunk, the aircraft-carrier *Courageous* later in the month, and in October the battleship *Royal Oak* while apparently safe in Scapa Flow. A British naval victory in the South Atlantic in December brought cheering news in time for Christmas: three British cruisers, though inferior in gun power, fought and damaged the pocket-battleship *Graf Spee*. Taking refuge in neutral waters at the mouth of the River Plate, the Germans scuttled their ship rather than come out to fight again.

While it was still quite uncertain how the state of war would develop, either in the direction of a patched-up political settlement or into a major campaign or campaigns, Russia made a surprise move in the north: on November 30th the Red army and air force attacked Finland. The Finns resisted bravely behind their Mannerheim Line, and held up the Russian advance. Russia was expelled from the League of Nations, and Britain and France considered sending a small force to aid Finland. But Norway and Sweden dared not prejudice their neutrality by allowing such a force to pass through their territory, and the scheme was abandoned. Russia at last forced the Finns to give way, and to hand over military bases and territory of strategic value. Russia's action could be explained—and was defended by Communists—on the ground that she must protect herself by putting buffers between herself and Germany. The like argument was used to defend Russian occupation of half of Poland and of the Baltic states of Estonia, Latvia and Lithuania. Yet, at the same time, Russia was on the best of terms with the Nazi aggressor, and Communists were loudly accusing Britain and France of being engaged in an imperialist war.

Hitler Overwhelms Denmark and Norway

But Finland was a pointer to coming events in that a large part of Scandinavia was soon to be involved in the war. Norway was a temptation to the Nazis: the long Norwegian coastline offered bases for U-boats and warships and for an extension of German air power; and, even more important, Germany bought iron ore from the north of Sweden and had, when the Swedish coast was frozen in winter, to bring the ore by train to the Norwegian port of Narvik, and ship it south through Norwegian territorial waters. To prevent this, the British laid mines, announced on April 8th, 1940, in Norwegian waters. The next day the previously launched and long prepared Nazi attack struck at Denmark and Norway. The attack was bold, determined and cunning. Denmark was at once overwhelmed. To reach Norway, the Germans had to cross the sea, but air power enabled them to do this, for Britain did not dare to risk her navy in the Skagerrak. The Germans seized most of the ports and airfields on the first day, and reinforcements poured in. The Norwegians resisted; an Allied force was sent to help them, but it had to be taken off in a fortnight. Only in the far north did the Allies win a success, when the navy destroyed the German ships at Narvik and enabled a land force temporarily to occupy the town. The King of Norway and his government escaped to England, with much important Norwegian shipping.

Blitzkrieg: Germany Over-runs the West: Churchill

There was, after these events, scarcely a breathing-space. On May 10th the real war began: Germany attacked the neutral countries of Belgium, Holland and Luxembourg—without warning, and with overwhelming forces by air and land —and all this was but the prelude to attack on France itself. Very soon the threat was apparent, not only to this or that small country, but to the whole Allied position.

On the same day that Germany attacked in the west, Britain found a new leader. Neville Chamberlain, "the man of Munich", had lost the confidence of parliament; as a result of Allied failure in Norway, he resigned, and Winston Churchill took his place as Prime Minister. At once, Churchill showed a new spirit—the spirit of indomitable, bulldog courage, which would never let go. Three days after the attack in the west, he warned parliament:

> I have nothing to offer but blood, toil, tears, and sweat. We have before us an ordeal of the most grievous kind. We have before us many long months of struggle and suffering. You ask, What is our policy? I will say: It is to wage war, by sea, land and air, with all our might and with all the strength that God can give us: to wage war against a monstrous tyranny, never surpassed in the dark, lamentable catalogue of human crime.

The German *Blitzkrieg* went ahead with overwhelming mechanised force and bewildering speed. The air force struck first, dive bombers attacked the Allied land forces, and bombing attacks also dislocated communications in the rear, spread alarm and panic, and filled the roads with refugees who impeded the movement of troops. Tanks and mechanised infantry moved up, to break their way through the opposing forces and, once through, to move ahead at an almost incredible rate. The Allied forces were cut in two, when the main German attack broke through near Sedan (the Maginot Line was by-passed, for it defended France's frontier with Germany, whereas along the Belgian frontier only superficial defences existed, put up by the B.E.F. during the winter). By May 18th German armoured forces reached Amiens, and two days later they reached the sea. To the north the B.E.F. and French forces which had moved forward into Belgium to meet the advancing Germans were cut off from the French armies to the south. Dutch resistance was all but over by May 14th, and on May 17th the Belgian King surrendered. The trapped British and French forces withdrew to the coast at Dunkirk. What appeared a miracle took place: the German pursuit slackened, there was good weather, and British naval superiority and the help of the R.A.F. from home bases made possible the evacuation of 335,000 British and Allied troops (though their equipment had to be abandoned) in a motley array of vessels, 200 naval vessels and some 600 other ships. Evacuation was completed by June 3rd.

To the south, General Weygand attempted to form a new line of defence along the Somme and the Aisne. But he was quite unable to hold up the German advance: on June 7th German tanks crossed the Somme, and on June 10th they crossed the Seine near Rouen. On the same day, emboldened by German victory, Italy entered the war on the German side. Four more days—and the Germans entered Paris (to save the city from destruction the French did not defend it). The country was falling into chaos, as the German bombers attacked the long lines of refugees, soldiers and civilians, streaming away along the roads. Parliament gave way to a dictatorship under Pétain, the First World War hero of Verdun, and on June 22nd France signed an armistice. France was out of the war, the north and west were occupied by German troops, Hitler spoke of a new order which would last a thousand years, and it looked to many people the world over as if Britain could not survive.

The Battle of Britain

But the British people did not flinch or hesitate. Churchill on June 18th spoke to parliament, and then broadcast to the nation:

What General Weygand called the Battle of France is over.

SECOND WORLD WAR
1939 - 1945

NORWAY

SWEDEN

FINLAND

LONDON

POLAND
• WARSAW

BERLIN •
GERMANY

PARIS
FRANCE

VIENNA
SWITZ-
ERLAND
AUSTRIA
HUNGARY
BUDAPEST

RUMANIA

YUGOSLAVIA
BELGRADE

ITALY
• ROME

BULGARIA

PORTUGAL

MADRID
SPAIN

Gibraltar (Br)

MOROCCO

ALGERIA

• Malta (Br)

L I B Y A

Greatest expansion of
German - Italian Power
Vichy France

0   100 200 300 400 500   Miles

SECOND WORLD WAR
1939 – 1945

Greatest expansion of
German – Italian Power

FINLAND

LENINGRAD

MOSCOW

POLAND

KIEV   KHARKOV   STALINGRAD

RUMANIA

BLACK SEA

UNION OF
SOVIET SOCIALIST
REPUBLICS

CASPIAN SEA

ISTANBUL

TURKEY

CRETE   CYPRUS   SYRIA
                              IRAQ

EL ALAMEIN   CAIRO

PERSIA

PERSIAN GULF

RED SEA

0   100 200 300 400 500
                              Miles

I expect that the Battle of Britain is about to begin. Upon this battle depends the survival of Christian civilisation. . . . Hitler knows that he will have to break us in this island or lose the war . . . if we fail, then the whole world, including the United States, including all that we have known and cared for, will sink into the abyss of a new Dark Age. . . . Let us therefore brace ourselves to our duties, and so bear ourselves that, if the British Empire and its Commonwealth last for a thousand years, men will still say, "This was their finest hour".

Under its indomitable leader the whole nation prepared for resistance; the Home Guard, a volunteer force, was formed. Allied men and ships which could be saved from France were brought to Britain, and General de Gaulle set up his Free French movement in this country.

The Battle of Britain began in July, and was fought out in the air. Victory in the air was necessary to the Germans before they could attempt invasion. If they could first destroy the R.A.F., then their bombing planes would be free to bomb British ports and cities by day, to attack and perhaps cripple the ships of the navy, and so to make an invasion of Britain by German armies little more than a follow-up operation. The air battles were the prelude: the Germans bombed the airfields, and attacked the British fighters in the air. Throughout August and September the outcome remained in doubt— aerial battles went on daily over the south-east of England. Britain was fortunate in having a splendid new fighter, the Spitfire, just coming into mass production, and also in having developed radar. Radar, which gave advanced warning of approaching enemy aircraft, enabled our limited numbers of planes to be sent to concentrate at the right points instead of having to disperse in prolonged patrolling. Of the fighter pilots themselves Churchill spoke in memorable terms: "Never in the field of human conflict was so much owed by so many to so few." On September 7th the Germans made their first night bombing attack on London; they kept it up for many weeks, and made heavy raids on other cities also. The *Blitz* brought its own terrors, and put a heavy strain on civilians. But the change to night bombing showed that Germany had failed to win the Battle of Britain.

The future, however, was uncertain, for Britain stood alone in Europe. Nevertheless Britain was allowed to draw more and more on American resources. In 1935 and 1937 the United States had, indeed, passed Neutrality Acts forbidding the export of arms and ammunition to a belligerent. But these laws were allowed to give place to a policy of "cash and carry"; if Britain could pay, and send ships, she could have munitions. Then, late in 1940, President Roosevelt let Britain have fifty destroyers in exchange for bases on British Caribbean islands. Early in 1941 "Lend-lease" was introduced; the U.S. lent supplies of war material and sent them over in American ships. Britain stood alone, but she was able to fortify herself for battles still to come. Hitler, too, had to consider the future. He had won tremendous and spectacular triumphs, but he had not succeeded in winning a quick victory over Britain. Hitler began again to look east, for his principal aim, consistently-held ever since his early days when he wrote *Mein Kampf,* was the conquest of Russia.

The War Spreads: Italy, North Africa, the Balkans

But first his ally Italy carried the war into north Africa. Italy had waited for the Nazi victory in France to enter the war; and, now that the Italian north African colony of Libya was freed by the French collapse from any danger of attack from the French colony of Tunis on its west, the Italians were free to move east against the British forces in Egypt. The Italians invaded Egypt on September 12th, and advanced some way. But in December, General Wavell with an imperial force, Indian, South African, Australian and New Zealand as well as British, struck back. He drove the Italians out of Egypt, destroyed their army, and made a spectacular advance into Libya, reaching Benghazi in February 1941.

But brilliant and encouraging as was Wavell's victory, the British position in the Near East was precarious. Germany during the winter of 1940–1 extended her power in the Balkans by diplomatic and economic pressure: German troops were allowed to enter Rumania, and Germany to prepare airfields in Rumania and Bulgaria. In October 1940, Italy attacked Greece—from bases in Albania which country Italy had seized in the spring of 1939. Italy expected an easy victory over the Greeks, but the Greek dictator, General Metaxas pushed them back. In April 1941, Hitler came to the rescue of the Italians. German forces attacked both Yugoslavia and Greece, and although a small British force had been sent to Greece, the Germans soon overcame resistance in both countries, the British escaping only with considerable loss. Next, in May, the Germans captured the island of Crete from the British by air attack; the island was strongly defended, but the defences were overwhelmed by bombing, together with the landing of parachutists and glider-borne troops. Thus the Germans secured their domination over the Balkans, and established a hold in the eastern Mediterranean; during the spring and summer, however, the Italians lost their colonies of Eritrea, Somaliland and Abyssinia, conquered by British and Indian troops. The Emperor Haile Selassie was restored to his Abyssinian throne. But meanwhile Hitler had sent to north Africa the well-equipped *Afrikakorps* under a skilled and audacious commander, Rommel. Rommel attacked, and by the end of April pushed Wavell's army back into Egypt. Nor could Britain easily send convoys through the Mediterranean, for German airfields in Sicily made the passage dangerous. Thus Britain clung with difficulty to her positions in the Near East. At home the German night bombing had ceased for some weeks—what did this signify? Where would Germany move next? Through Spain, perhaps, to Gibraltar and Africa? Through Turkey southeastwards, to cut the Suez route to India? Or would the Nazis move against Russia?

Germany Attacks Russia, 1941

The German armies attacked Russia, on June 22nd, 1941, along a vast front stretching for over a thousand miles. At one stroke, the whole outlook of the war changed: Britain was no longer alone; a powerful ally was at last in the struggle. Churchill immediately broadcast an announcement of British co-operation with Russia. Relative to her size, indeed,

Russia was weak, but nevertheless the Germans had undertaken a heavy task in embarking on the conquest of a country of 200 million people. Men remembered, too, the fate of Napoleon's army in 1812. At any rate Britain had been offered a breathing-space, much needed and well-earned; indeed, throughout the remaining years of the war Russia engaged about two-thirds of the German Army.

At first the German forces advanced rapidly. Their superiority in aircraft and tanks made this possible, and the Russians withdrew before the Germans could bring about any large-scale encirclement; by avoiding encirclement the Russian generals managed to maintain their huge armies largely intact. The German armoured forces advanced in three great thrusts: by the winter, the Northern Army Group was threatening Leningrad, and the city suffered what was almost a siege for over two years—but was never captured; the Centre Army Group moved towards Moscow, reached its outskirts in December, but was checked; the Southern Army Group moved through the Ukraine, captured the important cities of Kiev and Kharkov, and pushed on towards Rostov-on-Don.

Japan Attacks U.S.A.

In December 1941, there took place another tremendous event, perhaps more important even than the German attack on Russia: Japan made war on the United States. On December 7th, Japanese planes flown from air-craft carriers surprised the American Pacific Fleet at Pearl Harbor, Hawaii, and, in a matter of minutes, put it out of action. The European war at once changed to a global conflict; Germany and Italy declared war on America, and Britain declared war on Japan. It would seem that Japan and Germany made major errors of political strategy as Stalin had done in 1940. Stalin failed to attack Germany, when the German armies were fully engaged in the invasion of France. The Russian armies launched against Germany at that time might have saved France, would almost certainly have saved the French Empire in north Africa for the Allied cause; Stalin would have had the "second front" he demanded so persistently later on;

there would have been a two-front war from the start. Now Japan blundered in attacking the United States, whereas she could bit by bit have seized the French, Dutch and British possessions in the Far East *without* involving America. Instead of attacking the United States Japan might have made a surprise attack on Russia, and Germans and Japs would have met on the Trans-Siberian railway, as the Nazi foreign minister, Ribbentrop, had urged. Germany, too, blundered in declaring war on the United States; Germany could have left Japan to fight America, and so have avoided the vast American build-up in the west which ultimately proved fatal to Germany. Time was now on the Allies' side; they had superiority in numbers, resources and the means of producing munitions. Given time, they must win. But the next months were, nevertheless, a desperate period for the Allies, for the Japanese surprise blow gave them immense immediate advantage.

The Japanese secured control of the Pacific almost at once; within three days of Pearl Harbor their aircraft sank the British battleships the *Prince of Wales* and the *Repulse*—a shattering blow. Japanese power spread over the Far East at incredible speed; Britain lost Malaya, Singapore, Hong Kong and Burma, and at the same time important sources of tin and rubber. China (at war with Japan since 1937) was isolated by the Japanese cutting of the Burma road. India and Australia were menaced. But the United States reacted strongly to Pearl Harbor. That disaster was, perhaps, a blessing in disguise. America was galvanised into action: steadily and rapidly she built up immense forces. In May and June 1942, the Americans won two great naval victories, the Battle of the Coral Sea and the Battle of Midway Island, both fought by carrier-borne aircraft, without the fleets sighting each other or firing a shot. The Japanese were checked.

During the summer of 1942, on the whole, events were still moving in favour of Germany. Allied shipping resources were strained to the uttermost by the U-boats, the Atlantic communications were threatened, and in eastern waters the Japanese submarines were a persistent menace. Meanwhile, however, Britain was hitting back at Germany directly: bombing raids had begun in 1940, and were stepped-up in intensity. On May 30th, 1942, the R.A.F. carried out the first 1,000 bomber raid, on Cologne. The Russian winter of 1941–2 had done what, so far, Allied armies had failed to do; it checked the Nazi *Blitzkrieg*. The Germans were caught without proper winter clothing; frost-bite as well as the enemy caused severe loss of men. In the vast spaces of Russia, too, even the superb German army found itself up against difficulties of communication and supply; the forces had to reconstruct thousands of miles of Russian railways and set up huge supply depots. But when the spring came, the Germans advanced once more, in the south: they cleared the Crimea, sent one army into the Caucasus towards the oil-wells, and sent another eastwards to the Volga, where it set siege to Stalingrad. In north Africa, also, the Germans had had the better of it. The rival armies had ranged back and forth along the coastal strip several times. In June 1942, Rommel made his most formidable attack, and chased the British right back to El Alamein. It looked as if Rommel might over-run the British positions, break through to Alexandria, and seize control of Egypt.

The Tide Turns: Alamein, Stalingrad

But during the autumn and winter of 1942–3 the whole tide of war turned. In Egypt, during the summer, General Alexander and General Montgomery had built up a powerful attacking force. General Montgomery's Eighth Army attacked at El Alamein on October 23rd. In his personal message to the army before the battle Montgomery declared:

When I assumed command of the Eighth Army I said that the mandate was to destroy *Rommel* and his army, and that it would be done as soon as we were ready.

We are ready *now*.

The battle which is about to begin will be one of the decisive battles of history. It will be the turning-point of the war. The eyes of the world will be on us, watching anxiously which way the battle will swing.

We can give them their answer at once: "It will swing our way." Let us pray that "the Lord mighty in battle" will give us the victory.

Montgomery's confidence was justified. This time the Germans were heavily defeated, and the long pursuit through north Africa began again, now for the last time. On November 8th, too, the Allies landed large British and American forces under General Eisenhower in the French colonial territory of Morocco and Algeria. Thus Rommel was threatened from the west, as well as by the advancing British from the east. In Russia also the tide had turned. The Red army launched a counter-offensive on November 19th; it saved the ruins of Stalingrad, and eventually destroyed the German army besieging it, taking prisoner Field Marshal von Paulus (January–February 1943). Now at last the Allies had the upper hand: planes, tanks, weapons and munitions of all kinds were being provided in immense numbers; supplies were poured into Russia by the Arctic convoys and through Persia. Hitler had lost his start, and the Allies had caught him up. In January 1943, Churchill and Roosevelt met at Casablanca, and made plans directed towards the unconditional surrender of the enemy.

Following up their victory at Stalingrad, the Russians advanced. The Germans in the Caucasus, their rear threatened, had to extricate themselves, but they did so in orderly fashion, through Rostov and across the Kerch Strait. The Germans were still powerful, and in the spring regained some ground, including Kharkov, which they had lost in February.

In north Africa, also, the Germans in retreat showed themselves stubborn and able fighters; from time to time they staged well-planned surprises or counter-attacks. They postponed Allied victory in north Africa as long as possible: from south Italy a large German force got over by sea and air into Tunisia, seized the principal ports ahead of the Allied advance from the west, and repulsed Eisenhower's advancing forces. The Germans in Tunisia built up a strong position, and were reinforced by Rommel's retreating army on their east. The Germans were firmly established by the end of January 1943. Although pressed from west and east, it was not until May that the end came; the German and Italian prisoners amounted to 250,000 men. The whole of north Africa thus passed under Allied control, and the Mediterranean was open once more to Allied shipping.

War at Sea: U-Boat Peril

On other seas, meanwhile, and in the air, a relentless struggle went on. The German submarines were a lasting peril to Allied shipping, but occasionally a surface ship would escape from a German-occupied port and endanger whole convoys with destruction. Thus in May 1941, the *Bismarck* broke out into the north Atlantic. In a brief encounter it sank the battle-cruiser *Hood*. A desperate air and sea chase ensued, and at last the *Bismarck,* perhaps the strongest battleship in the world, was sunk. The submarines fought a continuous fight against our vital supply lines to America—and, since Ireland was neutral, we could not use the former naval bases there. The Battle of the Atlantic, as the prolonged struggle was known, might have won the war for Germany. The worst period was 1942–3. After that anti-submarine devices, including the new radar, gave the upper hand to the Allies. In the air R.A.F. bombers were carrying on steadily with the heavy bombing of industrial areas in Germany and Italy. From the summer of 1942 American bombers joined them; the British worked by night, the Americans by day. The scale of raids and the weight of bombs increased. The raids on Germany were far heavier than those on London and other British cities in the earlier part of the war. But even so German industry was never crippled. It has been suggested that some of the effort given to the bombing might have been better given to other things, such as the anti-submarine campaign or close support of the armies in the field. But this is a controversial matter over which experts still argue.

Allies Invade Sicily and Italy

When once they had cleared up the Germans in north Africa, the Allies were soon ready to use their new positions as bases from which to cross the Mediterranean and make the first attack on Europe. In July 1943, Allied forces landed in Sicily, and secured full possession of the island by the middle of August. The Allied success in Sicily brought the downfall of Mussolini; a new government was set up, and Italy surrendered. The collapse of Italian fascism did not, in fact, mean as much as it might, for the Germans with great resolution at once took over in Rome; they disarmed the remaining Italian forces. In September, the Allies landed in Italy itself. This seemed to follow naturally from the occupation of Sicily, but actually there were disagreements as to strategy. The Americans favoured immediate invasion of France, but against this was lack of time to complete the necessary preparations. But the Allied landings—north of Reggio and in the Bay of Salerno—were but the beginnings of a long campaign. The Germans fought back strongly, and the Allied way into Italy was stoutly contested; the Allies had to fight their way northwards in face of determined opposition. They captured Naples on October 1st. The Germans then stabilised their position and established fortified lines across Italy, south of Rome, from coast to coast. The old monastery of Monte Cassino, high on a hill, strongly fortified, and tenaciously defended by the Germans, held up the Allied advance from January to May 1944.

Other Allied Advances

In July 1943, the Russians took the offensive. During the summer and the winter of 1943–4 their advances continued, and they recovered much ground. By March 1944, they were back on the borders of Poland and Rumania. In the same winter of 1943–4 the Americans were extending their recovery in the Pacific by the capture of islands; the capture of Saipan in the summer of 1944 brought them within bombing range of Japan. By February 1944 the British army in Burma was achieving victory in some of the most difficult country in the world.

Allied Invasion of Normandy: "D" Day

Meanwhile the Allies had been preparing for the invasion of Germany from the west. The Allied leaders met a number of times in conference: Churchill went to Moscow in 1942; Churchill, Roosevelt and Stalin met at Teheran in 1943. Teheran decided the three-front attacks on Germany to take place in 1944. The failure in the summer of 1942 of the large-scale Canadian raid on Dieppe—which scarcely got beyond the beach—had shown how costly an assault on a defended coastline could be. In spite of initial American eagerness to invade as soon as possible, and in spite of repeated angry demands from Russia for a second front, the Allied leaders had put off the invasion date until 1944. Not until then, it was reckoned, would the preparations be complete. Planning staffs were busy for many months. Elaborate and comprehensive plans had to be made: to train and collect large forces ready for invasion, to provide equipment and supplies, to collect landing craft and shipping, and to arrange not only for the assault across the Channel but also to keep the forces supplied with all their many needs. In particular, petrol had to be supplied for the thousands of planes, tanks and motor vehicles. The problem was solved by the use, after the landings, of PLUTO—pipeline under the ocean—a prefabricated flexible pipe laid across the Channel bed. During the months before invasion intensive bombing was carried out both to dislocate, as far as possible, the German industrial system which supplied the German armies, and also to destroy bridges, railways and roads in northern France so as to cut communications and hinder enemy troops movements. Throughout the spring and early summer of 1944 the skies of southern England and nothern France were hardly ever silent by day or night.

In all, three major Allied advances came in the summer. First was the advance in Italy. In May General Alexander broke through the German lines and advanced northwards; Rome was liberated on June 4th. Next was the invasion of France.

On "D" Day, June 6th, 1944, the great invasion of France started under the command of General Eisenhower, with Montgomery in charge of the land forces. American, British and Canadian forces were carried across the Channel—by 4,000 ships under a huge "umbrella" of aircraft—and landed safely on the beaches of Normandy. Airborne divisions were towed over by gliders. After some hard fighting, the Allies secured their position. Then, while Montgomery's British army stood firm at Caen, the Americans on his right took Cherbourg, advanced rapidly through western Normandy, and then swung round to catch the Germans in a huge trap, the Falaise pocket. When they had cleared up all the Germans in this area, the Allies were free to advance across northern France. Paris was liberated by Free French troops in August. British and Canadian forces moved north-east, along the Channel coast and destroyed the sites from which the Nazis had been sending their flying bombs and rockets against London and southern England. These new weapons—Hitler's secret weapon—had started just after the Allied invasion. It was indeed fortunate that the Germans had not developed these dangerous and terrifying weapons earlier. As it was the Allied invasion was made just in time to allow the destruction of their sites before they could become a really serious menace to England.

The third big attack came on the Russian front, starting on June 23rd. The Russian advance was spectacular, and covered great distances. In July some German generals tried to kill Hitler with a bomb which exploded at his headquarters behind the eastern front. But the plot failed, and the Germans went on fighting bravely and stubbornly. The Russian advance continued, reaching the confines of Warsaw and East Prussia. In the west the Allied forces proceeded to liberate Belgium, and then to the more difficult task of freeing Holland. A big British-American airborne landing at Arnhem in September—with the aim of establishing a bridgehead across the Rhine and at the same time isolating the German army in Holland—failed. But the Allies were approaching German territory all along Germany's western frontier. The Germans, nevertheless, fought steadily, and still had spirit enough for a strong counter-attack. Just before Christmas, their commander in the west, von Runstedt, acting on the orders of Hitler, gathered his forces for a surprise attack with the possible objective of a break right through the Allied positions so cutting off the American and British forces from each other. He struck in the Ardennes (in southeast Belgium) and found a weak spot in the American lines. The German tanks went through—for a fortnight the Allies had an anxious time—but at length the German forces were stopped, and the Allied line restored. It was the last German effort.

Invasion of Germany, Death of Hitler, and Unconditional Surrender

In March 1945, the Allied forces crossed the Rhine—they found one bridge the Germans had failed to blow up at Remagen. By the end of April, the British and Americans had destroyed or captured the remaining German armies. Meanwhile the Russians had advanced from the east: Russians and Americans met on April 26th, and the Russians entered Berlin. Hitler shot himself in his underground bunker in the capital: Mussolini, in Italy, had already been captured and killed by anti-fascist partisans. So long as Hitler lived, the Germans obeyed and had gone on fighting. Now that he was dead they surrendered unconditionally, on May 7th, 1945.

Atom Bombs and Surrender of Japan

Hitler's *Reich*—the empire he had boasted would last a thousand years—was gone. But Japan remained to be defeated, and there was nothing to suggest to the public a speedy end of the war in the Far East. Freed from commitment in the west, however, the Allied effort could be stepped up against the Japanese. The Americans—now with vast air and naval strength—had already intensified their policy of "island-hopping"; their landings were fiercely contested by the Japanese, but they brought the Americans nearer to the Japanese mainland. The British had advanced in Burma, capturing Mandalay in March and Rangoon early in May. British troops had been poured into India, in order to prepare for an invasion of Malaya. Japan itself was under direct attack, from the air and from the sea—Britain's most powerful battleships were in Far Eastern waters now, and joined the American navy in shelling the coasts of Japan. But there still remained the carrying out of invasion of Japan itself before victory could be secured. It has been maintained since that Japan was ready to surrender in any case. But the Americans now had a weapon ready—new and of terrifying destructive power: the atom bomb. On August 6th, the first atom bomb was dropped on Hiroshima, killing some 87,000 people. A second bomb was dropped on August 9th on Nagasaki—and this brought Japanese surrender within a few days. The last of the great aggressors had been conquered: Hitler and Mussolini were dead, Germany, Italy and Japan had all been vanquished, the greatest war in history was over. Britain had survived—but in the course of the long and exhausting conflict, much in the world had changed, and new problems and new perils stood ahead.

11

After the War: A New World

THE TRANSITION FROM war to peace was made more smoothly than in 1918. In 1945 the fighting came to an end in two stages—first in Europe and then, three months later in the Far East, and, in any case, it had been evident for some time that the Allies had the upper hand, in the west at least, and that victory would not be long delayed. A good deal of thought had been given to the problems of transition: while the war system was going full blast, and every available man and woman was either in the forces or working in war industry, the peacetime problem of unemployment had disappeared. But would peace bring it back? A wit had spoken of "the danger of peace breaking out". The danger was foreseen, however: wartime controls were retained; food, clothes and sweets were still rationed to make a fair share available to all and to prevent inflation; and a system of demobilisation based on length of service worked smoothly and avoided the disturbances which followed the armistice of 1918.

But, at the same time, men faced problems of a new kind; they faced, in effect, a new world. To some extent, this was true after each war. But the changes which marked life after the Second World War were greater and more fundamental than those after the First. In Great Britain there was a swing to the left in politics. No one wanted to return to the economic depression and unemployment of the 1930s; people wanted something better than they had had before the war. So, in spite of the immense personal popularity of Churchill, the General Election of July 1945, gave a sweeping victory to the Labour Party under Clement Attlee. The pre-war years had seen two short Labour governments, but without power because dependent upon Liberal votes. Now, the Liberal Party was reduced to twelve. Labour, with nearly 400 members in the House of Commons, was for the first time in power.

Outside Britain, Europe was devastated and much of the Far East was in ferment. European countries needed economic assistance, while Eastern countries, no longer willing to tolerate European control, were demanding independence. Germany had surrendered unconditionally: her cities were in ruins; foreign armies from east and west had met on her territory. First Germany had to be dealt with—by Allied military government. Then there was a need for some new world organisation to take the place of the old League of Nations. But Europe was no longer what it had been: whereas the European powers had still dominated the scene, at least the European scene, in the 1920s and '30s, now two world powers, America and Russia, overshadowed all. Soon the tension between them, the cold war, would give its own special character to the political scene. Peoples and nations in India, in the Far East, and in Africa, were calling, or would soon call, for independence.

There was, too, something which was altogether new. The dropping of the atomic bombs on Japan made clear to all the presence of a new scientific factor. The use of atomic weapons in future might mean the destruction of mankind. Thus the principles of peace and war had to be rethought; statesmen and national leaders must re-examine lines of action which once had seemed possible and advantageous, and think out new methods of negotiation and compromise. The weapons of the Second World War were more destructive than those of the First, those of the First World War more deadly than those of previous wars, but *never* had there been anything to be compared with the new atomic weapon.

Settlement of the Enemy Powers

The Allies had foreseen that Germany must be occupied and placed under military government. At the Yalta Conference in February 1945, a provisional scheme was worked out, and this was completed at the Potsdam Conference—the final agreement being signed on August 2nd, by which time Attlee had replaced Churchill as Prime Minister. By this agreement supreme power in Germany was transferred to the governments of the four principal Allies—the U.S.A., Russia, Britain and France. It was to be exercised by the four commanders-in-chief in a Control Council, meeting in Berlin. Germany was divided into four zones of occupation, American, Russian, British and French, and the city of Berlin, which lay within the Russian zone, was treated separately, being divided into four sectors. Although the intention was that Germany should be governed as a whole, in fact each zone operated separately. Certain general principles were laid down at Potsdam—disarmament and demilitarisation of Germany, and also deindustrialisation so far as military production went; the destruction of the Nazi Party and all its organisations, and the prevention of all Nazi or militarist activity; the eventual reconstruction of German political life on a democratic basis—though this later term was differently interpreted by Russia and the Western Allies. In Austria too, as in Germany, a four-power occupation was imposed. But the Allied attitude to Austria was different; it was recognised that Germany had annexed Austria by force in 1938. The Allies, therefore, were prepared to recognise an Austrian government, and, in spite of Russian attempts to set up a Communist-controlled one, free elections resulted in victory for a party of the Roman Catholic Right. A new Austrian government, containing also members of other parties, was eventually recognised by Russia and the Western Allies, and allowed a fairly free hand.

The four Allies also agreed on a four-power tribunal at Nuremberg to try the major German war criminals. Of those tried, ten were executed in October 1946. Hitler, Goebbels and Himmler had died by suicide, and so escaped trial and execution. Göring, though condemned to death at Nuremberg, retained or obtained the means to poison himself while in his cell awaiting hanging.

About a peace treaty with Germany or Austria, Russia and the Western Allies could not agree. After hard bargaining, however, they did manage to agree to treaties with Italy and the lesser enemy powers (Rumania, Bulgaria, Hungary and Finland); these treaties were signed on February 10th, 1947. Disagreement increased, as time went on, between Russia and the Western Allies. Russia maintained a firm grip over Poland and the Balkan countries—satellites as they came to be called. It became impossible to work with Russia either in Germany or elsewhere. By 1949 the Western Allies agreed among themselves to the merging of their zones and the setting up of the West German Federal Republic, with its own German democratic government. The Russians also turned their zone into a puppet German state: there were no free elections: a German Communist government was simply set up. Since this was clearly the case, neither the Western Allies nor the German Federal Republic recognised it.

U.N.

After the First World War statesmen had created the League of Nations with the intention of preventing war in future. The intention had not been realised, but nevertheless a new league was set up in 1945. Churchill gave the idea his powerful support. Of the old League, in spite of the failures over Manchuria and Abyssinia, Churchill had said in 1938: "If the League of Nations has been mishandled and broken, we must rebuild it." Allied co-operation during the war had strengthened the idea of permanent co-operation. In 1944, Churchill said: "We must undoubtedly in our world structure embody a great part of all that was gained to the world by the structure and formation of the League of Nations. But we must arm our world organisation and make sure that, within the limits assigned to it, it has overwhelming military power." Thus it was that, after various discussions among the Allies, a general conference met at San Francisco from April to

June 1945, and drew up the charter of the United Nations, fifty-one nations being foundation members. This time America was closely associated from the start with the world organisation. The first General Assembly of the United Nations met in London in January 1946, but eventually New York became the new international headquarters.

U.N., as the new organisation came to be known for short, has a Security Council, General Assembly and international secretariat, machinery very similar to that of the old League of Nations. And the main function was, and is—as with the League—to deal with international disagreements in time, and so prevent war. In addition, again like the League, U.N. undertakes many social, economic and educational tasks—such as the care and resettlement of displaced persons and refugees after the war, and the giving of advice and assistance to undeveloped countries.

It appeared at first that U.N. had one great advantage over the League: from the start both America and Russia were members. But with the development of the rivalry between them, the cold war between democracy and Communism, the U.N. has often been brought to deadlock. To take action the great power members of the Security Council must agree; each of them has the right of veto, and this right Russia has frequently used. Thus Churchill's idea of a body with overwhelming military force has been nullified. U.N. is often fatally divided: a course of action proposed by and welcome to the West can be prevented by the Russian veto.

The Labour Government: Nationalisation and the Welfare State

The victory of the Labour Party in 1945 came as a surprise to many people, certainly to Churchill. To him it must have seemed that the decision of the electorate was base ingratitude; yet his defeat was not, as with Lloyd George in 1922, the end of his political career, and his return six years later shows that the electoral swing to Labour was not the result of political causes as profound as one might have supposed. But as the election results demonstrated people wanted and were ready for a change; it was felt that the centralised planning and the national organisation, together with the determination which had gone with them in winning the war, should now be applied to the problems of the peace. The Labour election manifesto *Let us Face the Future* had put forward clearly a planned transition from a war to a peacetime economy and a moderate programme of nationalisation.

Grave economic difficulties faced the new government. What Great Britain owed to foreign countries (in spite of lend-lease and sales of British investments abroad) had greatly increased. There had been a heavy loss of shipping from wartime sinkings, some 5,000,000 houses had been destroyed or damaged in the bombing, and industry had suffered depreciation in the state of its machinery, equipment and buildings. It was thought that if British exports could be raised by seventy-five per cent. the payments out and in could be balanced. J. M. Keynes, the economist, who had been busy during the war with Anglo-American arrangements for lend-lease and more recently with the founding of a world bank and international monetary fund to assist in maintaining stable currencies, was sent to the U.S.A. to negotiate a loan of 3,750 million dollars. This it was hoped would see Britain through the immediate difficulty until revived exports would allow her once more to pay her way. But, in spite of this loan, financial crisis was never far off; bread and potatoes were rationed; the extreme winter of 1946–7 led to difficulties in moving coal and temporary closing down of industry with consequent unemployment; in 1947 an acute situation forced the Chancellor of the Exchequer, Sir Stafford Cripps, to adopt measures of restriction (among them refusing foreign currency for travel and suspending the petrol ration) in order to cut down dollar imports and restore the balance of payments. At this point, however, America once more came to the rescue with large-scale financial aid to Europe, in which Britain shared.

The Labour Party for many years had had its socialist programme—the nationalisation of the means of production, distribution and exchange. Now, in 1945, it had at last its opportunity to put that programme into effect. The new government passed measures for the nationalisation of the

Bank of England, the mines, the railways, civil aviation, road transport, gas and electricity. Once, not so long before, these measures would have been thought revolutionary, but, now that people had grown in wartime more used to state control, they were quietly accepted. More controversial was the Labour plan to nationalise steel; this proposal was indeed hotly contested, for the steel industry was working efficiently—and when the Conservatives returned to office in 1951 they were able to prevent the Labour plan to nationalise steel being put into effect.

Has nationalisation been successful? This is the kind of question it is most difficult to answer. Nationalisation has clearly worked; it has not brought economic ruin—far from it—as many of the older, individualist critics of socialist proposals had argued. It has certain advantages in making possible co-ordination and large-scale planning. But compensation had to be paid to the former owners (the shareholders) of the nationalised industries. Nor did nationalisation bring, as many socialists had hoped and expected, workers' control of industry. The workers themselves do not control industry any more than they did in the days of private enterprise. The national boards set up are remote from the ordinary worker, and management consists of much the same people as before. Although conditions improved greatly—wages, hours and paid holidays—equality of incomes remained remote; the men at the head of nationalised industries had still to be paid very large salaries, at least as much as able men could gain in private enterprise. A few important trade unionists were put on the new public boards, but this did not transform a capitalist society into a socialist one.

At the same time the Labour government carried through most important measures of social welfare—so important, and so much giving their character to at least one sphere of post-war state activity, that the term "Welfare State" has come into common use. These measures, of course, were not by any means wholly new. Lloyd George had been the great pioneer in this field, and indeed Labour's social measures were based on the work of another Liberal, Lord Beveridge, who produced his famous *Report* during the Second World

War. In this report—produced in 1942 at the request of the wartime government—he put forward a model plan for the social services, to destroy what he called "five giants on the road of reconstruction": Want, Disease, Ignorance, Squalor and Idleness. His plan was "a plan of insurance—of giving in return for contributions benefits up to subsistence level, as of right and without means test, so that individuals may build freely upon it". In 1945 Family Allowances were made available by the wartime government to help parents with young families. With all this in mind the Labour government passed its measures. In 1946 the National Insurance Act was passed, and also the National Health Service Act (the work of Aneurin Bevan), both coming into operation in 1948. The National Insurance Act provided a comprehensive system under which everyone was to pay contributions into a state fund out of which financial help could be given to the sick, unemployed, bereaved women and children, and to the aged. In addition, there remained National Assistance to cover the need for any further help in especially difficult cases.) The National Health Service provided free medical and dental treatment, free hospital treatment when necessary, and, at first, free medicine, dentures and spectacles. The cost was heavy, and it was found necessary later to introduce some small charges in the case of dental treatment, and the provision of medicines and appliances.

There were other ways also in which additional state help was given to people in need. Infant welfare centres offered advice and assistance to mothers, and enabled them to get milk and other foods cheaply. Plans were set on foot, by central and local government, for repairing and rebuilding war-damaged dwellings and for building new houses and flats. And a great expansion took place of the educational system. The wartime government had passed the Education Act of 1944, and the Labour government saw that it was largely implemented. Thus in 1947 the school-leaving age was raised to fifteen. Under the Act all children went, free of charge, to some kind of secondary school—though, of course, it took time to provide the necessary accommodation and staff to make it possible. Eventually many more boys and girls stayed on in grammar schools until eighteen, and many more grants were made available for study at the universities. As a result there came about not only an expansion of schools but also of universities, technical schools and teacher training colleges.

The Labour government undoubtedly made possible a transition from a largely capitalist to at least a partly socialist state. It laid foundations for the future—foundations which later Conservative governments would accept as laid once and for all and on which they too could build. There was indeed a large measure of agreement among the parties —if the Liberals as a party had virtually disappeared they had done a great work in liberalising both Conservatives and Labour. Increased wages, shorter hours, full employment led in time to conditions of affluence—in the 1950s the term "affluent society" was heard as well as "Welfare State". But during the period of Labour government (1945–51) many shortages still existed; many things were rationed —sugar and tea until 1952, and meat, bacon, butter and fats until 1954. (Bread and potatoes were de-rationed in 1948, clothes and footwear in 1949.) There was also an acute housing shortage for some years. Shortages made people "fed up"—shortages in peacetime were much more resented than in wartime. "Spivs" began to operate a black market, making quick profits by offering at high prices rationed or otherwise unobtainable goods they had obtained illegally. These things contributed to a decline in the popularity of the Labour government.

Why are we Prosperous?

On the whole the years since the Second World War—in spite of financial crises—have been years of prosperity. To live in an affluent society has been a new experience for those who remember the world economic slump of the 1930s. Both the First World War and the Napoleonic Wars, a hundred years earlier, were followed by prolonged depression. But this phenomenon did not follow the Second World War. Instead came rapid recovery followed by growing prosperity, the most marked feature of which has been the maintenance of full employment. The percentage rate of unemployment in the United Kingdom has in only one year since 1946 risen as high as 2 per cent., whereas it rose to 15.6 in 1921, to 22.8 in 1932, and during the whole period 1921–38 never fell below 9.2 per cent. Full employment is indeed a truly remarkable characteristic of the new Britain. Over against this tremendous improvement must, of course, be put the evil of inflation: prices have risen threefold (since the 1930s). Thus the value of money has fallen, so that those who worked and saved in earlier days, and those who live on fixed incomes and pensions, are to some extent paying the cost of the present prosperity of the many. Even so, on balance, the improvement is very great: wages have increased considerably (even allowing for the increase in prices), and the resulting prosperity is widely spread over the greater part of the community. The economic improvement cannot, it seems, be attributed to the definite policy of any one party. The Labour Party, which was in power for the first difficult post-war years, succeeded in overcoming the immediate problems. But prosperity continued, and grew greater, under the Conservative government which followed. The Labour Party, perhaps, laid the foundations—but both parties or neither can claim credit for the economic progress which has resulted. Behind and independent of the political parties and their policies there have been important forces making for an increase in real wealth. Two such forces are technical progress, thanks to scientists and technologists, and the limitation of population making for smaller families, though both these factors have been operative throughout our whole period. But the Labour Party during the years 1945–51 gave a bias to economic development in the direction of greater equality of income. It was often said in the 1930s that the problem of unemployment was a problem of distribution, not of production. Technical progress had increased national income. Unemployment was paradoxical—poverty in the midst of plenty. The Labour government helped to make national wealth available to the whole community.

Certainly the United States made a very important contribution to world economic recovery. First came her immediate post-war loan to Britain (Britain also received a considerable loan from Canada): next came Marshall aid in 1948 and the

O.E.E.C.—economic assistance to Europe of a most generous kind and on a scale without precedent; then there was American help to other parts of the world also, to undeveloped countries in Asia and Africa. All this financial aid from America helped the European nations and others to supply themselves with capital equipment and necessities quickly, and so to get their economic life going again after the war. In this general recovery Britain shared.

British policy, more than ever before, was consciously directed to maintaining full employment by the greatest possible development of economic activity. At first, with the wartime example of successful large-scale military planning in mind, the emphasis was on economic planning—nationalisation and state control—but this proved difficult in peacetime when the government could not direct and order as it could in war. From about 1948 onwards there was a retreat from planning, and, more and more, monetary controls were used instead. Indeed, from the start, Treasury policy—directed by the Chancellor of the Exchequer, Hugh Dalton, the disciple of Keynes—had been one of cheap money and greatly increased government expenditure, calculated to develop industry and to provide employment. Military expenditure and social service expenditure—both measured as percentages of gross national product—increased greatly. Military expenditure by 1951 was double what it had been in the 1930s (and compulsory military service occupied young men in the services); expenditure on the social services (including education) increased by more than half. Then there was a building programme: pressure was put on local authorities to build houses, and they were helped with Treasury grants. Atomic energy was developed by the Atomic Energy Authority, and the British Electricity Authority undertook the building of atomic power stations. In agriculture, guaranteed prices to farmers and grants for improvements were given, all with government money. In the nationalised industries—and in private enterprise also, where there was vast expansion in the motor car, aeroplane, oil, electrical and chemical industries—wages were increased. All these things helped to give employment and spread a share of the national product to all classes.

In a way, it all sounds so easy. Economists speak of the Keynesian revolution—"we are all Keynesians now"—meaning very briefly, that there must be sufficient government expenditure to make use of savings which otherwise would remain unused in bank balances and so to maintain employment especially in times of threatening slump. The Keynesian doctrine is essentially one for a period of economic slump (though once full employment is achieved, lavish government expenditure will tend to produce inflation). Could we, then, have done in the 1930s what has been done in the post-war years? Roosevelt with the New Deal of state-provided public works and Hitler with gigantic rearmament both stumbled on what was a kind of Keynesian remedy for unemployment *before* Keynes had written his most important work, *The General Theory of Employment, Interest and Money*, in 1936. But long before that Keynes had been in search of a solution to the economic problem of the times, and he had taken a large share in formulating the *We can conquer Unemployment* policy of Lloyd George. It may well be that the real tragedy of those days was the failure of Lloyd George to win the election of 1929 when his unemployment policy was submitted to the electorate. Yet, even now, are we certain that we are in control of the economic system? How far are full employment and prosperity permanent features of the economic scene? These are questions which only the future can answer. It is curious, indeed, how little the questions are discussed today or how seldom even formulated; the younger generation which has grown up in an affluent society knows nothing of the prolonged economic depression of the 1920s and '30s.

Empire to Commonwealth

Just as the Labour government had taken measures which marked an economic transition, so it also initiated measures which led to very great changes in the structure of the British Empire. It was perhaps fortunate that, when many parts of the Commonwealth were looking for independence, the British people and the Labour government were ready for change. (Churchill's attitude was different—"What we have, we hold".) The changes, of course, had their antecedents in the past. The First World War had stimulated a demand for self-government; between the wars the Dominions emerged as equal, independent nations within the Commonwealth; the Second World War still further stimulated the demand for independence, and today we seldom speak of the Empire but instead of the Commonwealth. Other empires also have changed or disappeared. During the eighteenth and nineteenth centuries there was a great expansion of the European nations, through empire-building, into Asia and Africa. The post-war years, however, have seen a movement in the opposite direction, the retreat from Asia and Africa of the European empires.

Most spectacular was the British departure from India. There, in the once proud Indian Empire, people had clamoured for freedom, and it had become clear that Britain could not continue indefinitely to rule this huge territory against the will of its 400 million people. But the peoples of India, though they had caught the idea of freedom, were not united among themselves. They were divided, chiefly, into two great religious communities, Hindu and Moslem, often fanatically opposed to each other. Negotiations between Britain and the Indian leaders (Gandhi and Nehru for the Hindus, Jinnah for the Moslems) were arduous, and came near to breakdown. In the end, Attlee fixed a time-limit: by a fixed date, whatever happened, Britain would transfer power and responsibility to the Indian leaders. And so in August 1947, power was handed over to the two communities. Thus, instead of being one great country, India was divided into two states: India and Pakistan. The transfer did not come about without bloodshed. Massacres took place, in India of Moslems, and in Pakistan of Hindus; about a million lives were lost. But things might have been very much worse. In spite of the bitterness aroused, both the new countries soon settled down and took their new responsibilities seriously.

The end of the Indian Empire did not mean the ending of all relations with Britain. Indeed independence, so freely granted by Britain, brought a friendlier relationship, and both India and Pakistan chose to remain in the Commonwealth. In 1950 India became a republic, as did Pakistan also, though later on, in 1956; but each recognised the British monarch as Head of the Commonwealth. In 1948 Ceylon and Burma were granted independence; Ceylon remained in the Commonwealth, but Burma went her own way without the retention of this imperial link. All these countries, of course, have their troubles; people are not accustomed to democracy, and their economic condition in many places is one of great poverty. Burma has had civil war; in Pakistan dishonesty among politicians led in 1958 to the taking over of government by an army leader; in Ceylon there have been disturbances between Sinhalese and Tamils, and in 1958 some hundreds of people were killed. To replace British rule by a government equally strong and just was not easy.

In the Far East, the defeat of the Japanese at the end of the war saw British control restored in Malaya and Singapore. The existence of local inter-racial rivalries between the different nationalities, Malay, Chinese and Indian, made difficult the emergence of a simple anti-British nationalism. But Malaya had its own special trouble. For some years guerilla warfare was carried on in the jungles by Communists, mainly Chinese. Eventually the guerillas were overcome, and in 1957 Malaya attained independence with its own elective monarchy; Singapore achieved self-government in the following year.

In the Mediterranean, too, Britain had serious difficulties: there were grumblings in Malta, and prolonged terrorism in Palestine and in Cyprus. In 1947, after her long effort to maintain some kind of peaceful rule over Jews and Arabs, Britain gave up her mandate for Palestine, and the Jewish state of Israel came into existence. The Greek population of Cyprus were demanding union with Greece (*Enosis*), but there was a strong Turkish minority quite unwilling for this. To Britain the island was an important military base, but quite apart from this there was the danger of civil war between Greeks and Turks, if Britain left, and also of war between Greece and Turkey. Eventually, in 1959, an agreement was reached making Cyprus an independent republic.

Elsewhere, too, advances towards self-government have been going on, in the West Indies, and in Africa.

Britain has given financial aid for social and economic development, school systems have been expanded, and new universities founded. In Africa "the wind of change" blew strongly. Before the war even educated people took little interest in the African colonies, but by the 1950s names like Kenya, Uganda and Nigeria had become familiar in the news. More and more African students came to Britain to study, and British people went out to teach and work in the African territories. Everywhere the African people, living in territories undeveloped and poor, were striving for self-government and independence, and confronting Britain and the world with new problems. The Gold Coast, taking the name of Ghana, became independent in 1957; Nigeria achieved independence in 1960, and Tanganyika in 1961. Nigeria—with its 35 million people, the largest population of any African state—is the fourth largest Commonwealth country, after India, Pakistan and Britain. All these territories, African and Indian, had passed through a preparatory stage, in which people had been trained by British administrators and made ready to administer their own affairs. All have remained in the Commonwealth. In some parts of Africa, of course, there have been serious troubles. In Kenya in 1952 there was a barbarous outbreak called Mau Mau, which was directed against white men owning land there—the problem of a colony moving towards self-government is greatly complicated by the presence of white settlers. In 1953 the federation of Northern Rhodesia and Nyasaland with Southern Rhodesia provoked African opposition, for the Africans feared that they would be dominated by the whites of Southern Rhodesia. What happened in the Belgian Congo when it was given independence in 1960, showed only too clearly the dangers of premature self-government.

The movement in Africa towards self-government and economic development goes on, and must go on for many years to come. Self-government and prosperity cannot come all at once. Meanwhile the British Commonwealth is changing. South Africa withdrew in 1961 because its white government's policy of *Apartheid* or racial segregation was not acceptable to the other members. In population the coloured nations of the Commonwealth far outweigh the white; what was once an association of white Dominions has come to be one in which the whites could be over-ruled by Afro-Asian voices. But Commonwealth still stands for a great ideal, and a means to strength and mutual protection in a divided and dangerous world.

The great changes in Empire and Commonwealth which began with the Labour government after the war continued throughout the following period of Conservative government, and are still going on. They have therefore been dealt with here as a continuous story. We must now return to the late 1940s and observe the progress of the cold war which was a continuing threat to Britain and the Western world.

The Cold War and European Recovery

Churchill, when he visited the U.S. early in 1946, boldly warned the world against the Russian peril. Speaking at Fulton, Missouri, with President Truman presiding, Churchill made a strong appeal for continued Anglo-American co-operation, and spoke of the iron curtain which Russia had drawn down between the Communist countries and the West. The cold war, the struggle between Russia and the West, persisted, and has gone on, in one way or another, without cease. When the Communists finally won the civil war in China, China began to appear as a potential third world power, Communist and far larger than Russia itself. But for the time being Russia remained the principal Communist power, dominating, as she did, and leading her satellite powers, Poland, Hungary, Bulgaria, Rumania, Yugoslavia, Albania and East Germany. In March 1948, the Communists in Czechoslovakia seized control of the government, and that country passed under Russian influence. Then, later in the same year, the Russians made a strong effort to force the Western powers out of Berlin, control of which was shared by the four wartime Allies. The Russians blocked road and railway communications between West Germany and Berlin. For months America and Britain provisioned the city by an "air-lift", and eventually the Russians gave way. The threat to the West however, was great, and growing: there was a challenge in Communist totalitarianism to the whole democratic way of life.

To the constant pressure from Russia the West responded at first rather slowly and uncertainly. But at length the response was strong and definite. In 1948 a large scheme of American aid to Europe, the Marshall plan—so called after the American General Marshall who proposed it the previous year in a speech at Harvard—was put into effect, and O.E.E.C., the Organisation of European Economic Co-operation, was set up to run it. This helped Europe, including Britain, to get its economic life really going again, and to set it on the road to prosperity. For economic recovery in the struggle with Communism was as important as military defence, but in effect provisions for common defence were also pushed ahead. Britain and France signed a treaty in 1947, and in the following year agreed with Belgium, Holland and Luxemburg to the defence organisation of Western Union. But even then, it was realised that all would be in vain without American help, and at last the North Atlantic Treaty was signed in Washington in 1949. The U.S. and Canada joined with Britain, France, Belgium, Holland, Luxemburg, Italy, Portugal, Norway, Denmark and Iceland "to unite their efforts for collective defence for the preservation of peace and security" and agreed that "an armed attack against one shall be considered an attack against them all" (later on, in 1951, Greece and Turkey were added as members, and in 1954 the German Federal Republic). Thus N.A.T.O.—North Atlantic Treaty Organisation—came into existence. A council and other bodies were set up, and a network of commands, radar installations and airfields under S.H.A.P.E. (Supreme Headquarters Allied Powers, Europe). Other more purely European institutions also developed, such as the Council of Europe (1949), which its supporters hoped might become the foundation for a European government, and the European Common Market, beginning in 1951 with a coal, iron and steel authority and going on in 1957 to a wider common market of which in 1961 Britain was seeking membership. And in September 1962, the visit of the heroic French President, General de Gaulle, to the elderly but still dominant West German Chancellor Adenauer, suggested the possibility of a future closer political union of the two countries. Everywhere on his tour of West Germany, de Gaulle was welcomed by large and cheering crowds. Europe indeed was launched on a period of remarkable prosperity in the 1950s: West Germany became one of the most prosperous states, and in Britain people "had never had it so good". For the moment, the headlong career of Communism in Europe was checked.

But in the Far East the cold war became hot. Korea, formerly under Japan, had been divided into two zones of occupation, Russian and American. In 1950 Communist North Korea attacked South Korea from which American forces had only just withdrawn. This time the U.N. Security Council (owing to Russian absence) could agree to take action. U.N. forces, mainly American, were sent, and a British Commonwealth Division joined them. The war in Korea went on for three years, and ended at last with Korea still divided. With the death of Stalin in 1953 (which facilitated the making of peace in Korea) there was a slight thaw in the cold war. But Communist activities elsewhere in the Far East, and the ruthless Russian suppression of the free government set up in Hungary in 1956, made things worse again. Under Khrushchev, who emerged as the new Russian leader, there were, however, many more contacts—summit conferences between heads of state and also visits and tourism by ordinary people. Yet as late as 1961 there was a serious crisis over Berlin worked up by Khrushchev. After this, once again, there was a slackening of tension.

Such incidents will continue for many years, and perhaps as some statesmen say, for generations. For Communism has not given up its avowed intention of capturing the whole world, and as lately as 1959 Mr Khrushchev announced that he expected to see the Red Flag fly over every country of the world in his lifetime.

If the West was slow to recognize the menace of Communism, it is still slower to face the full dimension of its challenge. Communists might, of course, if the opportunity offered, back their aim with their maximum military power, though there are signs that for the moment they consider all-out nuclear war to be dangerous and have turned, as in

Viet Nam, to the "twilight land" of guerilla warfare and political subversion. They also use their economic resources to their greatest extent, buying and selling in world markets not for profit but for ideological purposes. But, above all, they put their trust in the ideological weapon. They believe that the future of the world goes to the people who win the hearts and minds of the masses. Lenin said that every division, every discontent, every bitterness, must be used for the furtherance of the Communist revolution, and in the postwar world these elements are common and are being sedulously exploited, not only in Africa and Asia where millions are underfed, but in the advanced industrial countries, and even in America and Britain.

For Communism is not so much a political party as an ideology which aims to take the place of God and replace every religion. It is making its supreme bid at a time when other faiths have declined and Western man too seldom feels as passionately for the spiritual foundations on which democracy was originally built as convinced Communists feel for their ideas. The future may depend on whether the balance can be redressed and the free world can find again a faith for which it will live and die.

Britain at Home and Abroad

In the elections of 1951 the Conservatives gained a small majority—Churchill returned as Prime Minister until he retired in 1955—and the Conservatives have remained in office since then; Eden followed Churchill, and on his retirement in 1957 was followed by Harold Macmillan. Home policy has not radically changed. The Conservatives have accepted most of the Labour government's reforms, and economic policy has continued to maintain full employment and prosperity. In 1952 King George VI died, after a brave struggle against serious illness. He had ruled with great devotion since 1936, when he had had, unexpectedly, to become King on the abdication of his brother, Edward VIII. George VI had no son, and so his elder daughter became Queen. As Elizabeth II she was hailed with enthusiasm. Just before her coronation in June 1953, came the news that a British expedition had climbed Mount Everest, hitherto unclimbed, the highest mountain in the world. During 1957–8 a British expedition crossed the Antarctic Continent overland. These exploits seemed to herald a new Elizabethan Age.

One event, however, shook Britain deeply, and divided opinion more sharply than ever before in recent times. This event was the Suez crisis of 1956. Eden, who remembered so well the rise of Hitler, thought he saw another, this time a Near Eastern Hitler, in the person of President Nasser of Egypt. Nasser had acted in a most high-handed manner: he had persuaded the British to give up their important military base in the Suez Canal region, and then he had seized the Canal (the property of an international company) and resisted all attempts at compromise. Eden took the opportunity of an Israeli attack on Egypt (for Israel also feared Nasser's ambitions as Leader of Arab nationalism), to launch with France an armed intervention: Egyptian airfields were bombed, and a force landed at Port Said. But the U.N. and world opinion were against England and France; there were threats from Russia. Britain and France gave way, and agreed to a U.N. force occupying the trouble spots while they withdrew. Eden's health failed and he gave up office. Personal tragedy and international crisis combined. The rights and wrongs were hotly debated in Britain as elsewhere. But it was remarkable how quickly the crisis passed. One thing, however, was clear: European powers like England and France no longer had the power of action they once had had.

In science and industrial advances Britain shared—and in some fields led—what was a common experience to the Western world and industrialised countries elsewhere. Unprecedented advances have been made. The end of the Second World War saw the first jet engines, and soon they came into use in civil aviation. Air travel became faster and easier. There were new materials, plastics; new synthetic fibres, nylon and terylene; new drugs, the sulpha drugs and penicillin. The tractor replaced the horse in farming; the combine harvester, long used in North America but first used in Britain only in 1928, became common in this country wherever farms are large. Most awe-inspiring of the new developments was that of atomic power. The threat of the bomb has hung, and still hangs, over the world. But atomic power has been harnessed for peaceful purposes also—Britain began and is continuing the building of atomic power stations to generate electricity. Atomic power offers a source of power, heat and light still available when existing sources such as coal and oil may be used up. At the same time Russia and America have competed in the development of rockets. The Russians sent up their first rocket to put a satellite into orbit round the earth in 1957—the satellite was launched from the third stage of the rocket. Several others, Russian and American, followed. In 1959 the Russians sent out a moon probe which passed the moon and went into orbit round the sun— the first artificial planet. Later that year another Russian rocket passed around the moon, and photographed its hidden side. Soon afterwards animals were sent up, and then in 1961 the Russians put up the first man, Major Gagarin, to orbit the earth. In February 1962, the Americans put up their Colonel Glenn. Both Russians and Americans look forward to sending men to the moon before 1970. In enterprises of this kind, vastly expensive, only Russia and America can compete.

Yet Britain still maintains her place not without power and influence. In the European Common Market, "assuming the accession of the United Kingdom", President Kennedy saw the prospect of a trading group with an economy nearly equal to the American.[1] In two world conflicts Britain has taken a leading and victorious part, and parliamentary democracy—above all a British development—is still a political model to much of the world, and to democracy the Communists themselves pay at least lip-service.

Britain now stands in a unique position between the two giants of Russia and America. If she can provide an answer in her own way of life to the materialism which in a different form haunts both West and East, she may yet play her greatest role and show a road away from world conflict.

[1] State of the Union Message. January 1962

Date Summary

	Home	Foreign and Imperial
1868–74	*Gladstone's first government* (Liberal)	
1869	Disestablishment of the church in Ireland	
1870	Irish Land Act	
	Elementary Education Act	
1871	University Tests Act	
	Abolition of purchase of commissions in the army	
1872	Ballot Act	
1874–80	*Disraeli's government* (Conservative)	
1875	Public Health Act	Disraeli bought the Khedive's shares in the Suez Canal Company
	Artisans' Dwellings Act	
	Trade Union Legislation (Conspiracy and Protection of Property Act)	
1875–85	Agricultural depression (and further depression 1891–9)	
1876		Queen Victoria became Empress of India
1878	Factories and Workshops Act	Congress of Berlin
		War with Afghanistan
1879		War with the Zulus
1880–5	*Gladstone's second government*	
1881	Disraeli died	Boers defeated British at Majuba Hill
	Second Irish Land Act	
1882		Gladstone intervened in Egypt
1884	Third Reform Act	
1885	*Lord Salisbury's first government* (Conservative)	Gordon killed at Khartoum
1886	*Gladstone's third government*	
	First Home Rule Bill defeated in House of Commons	
1886–92	*Lord Salisbury's second government*	Rapid expansion of Empire, especially in Africa

212

	Home	*Foreign and Imperial*
1887	Queen Victoria's Golden Jubilee	First Colonial Conference
1888	Local Government Act	
1889	London dock strike	Rhodes founded British South Africa Company —beginning of Rhodesia
1892–4	*Gladstone's fourth government*	
1893	Second Home Rule Bill defeated in House of Lords	
	Independent Labour Party founded	
1894–5	*Lord Rosebery's government* (Liberal)	
1895–1902	*Lord Salisbury's third government*	
1895–6		Jameson Raid
1896–8		Sudan reconquered
1897	Queen Victoria's Diamond Jubilee	Second Colonial Conference
1898		Fashoda
1899–1902		Boer War
1901	DEATH OF QUEEN VICTORIA	
1901–10	Edward VII	
1902–5	*Balfour's government* (Conservative)	
1902	Education Act	Treaty with Japan
1904		*Entente* with France
1905–8	*Campbell-Bannerman's government* (Liberal)	
1905		Morocco crisis
1906	Sweeping Liberal victory in General Election	
	Labour Party established in parliament	
1907	Trade Disputes Act	Triple Entente
1908		Crisis over Bosnia-Herzegovina
1908–16	*Asquith's government* (Liberal)	
1909	Lloyd George's Budget rejected by House of Lords	
1910–36	George V	
1911	Parliament Act	Second Morocco crisis
	National Insurance Act	
1912–13		Balkan wars
1913	Trade Union Act	
1914–18	FIRST WORLD WAR	
1915–16	*Asquith's second government* (Coalition)	
1916	Rising in Dublin (Easter)	
1916–22	*Lloyd George's government* (Coalition)	
1918	Representation of the People Act	
	Education Act	

	Home	*Foreign and Imperial*
1919		Treaty of Versailles
		League of Nations set up
1920	Beginnings of industrial depression and unemployment	
	Unemployment Insurance Act	
	Emergency Powers Act	
1921	Irish Free State created	
1922–3	*Bonar Law's government* (Conservative)	
1922		Mussolini came to power in Italy
1923–4	*Baldwin's first government* (Conservative)	
1924	*First Labour government* (Ramsay MacDonald)	
1924–9	*Baldwin's second government*	
1926	General Strike	Imperial Conference (Autonomy and equality of Dominions)
1929–31	*Second Labour government* (Ramsay MacDonald)	
1929		Panic on Wall Street (New York Stock Exchange). Beginning of World slump
1931	Economic crisis—MacDonald formed National Government	Statute of Westminster
		Japan attacked China
1931–40	*National Government:* under Ramsay MacDonald 1931–5	
	Baldwin 1935–7	
	Neville Chamberlain 1937–40	
1933		Hitler came to power in Germany
1935–6		Mussolini conquered Abyssinia
1936	Edward VIII Abdication Crisis	
1936–52	George VI	
1938		Hitler seized Austria
		Munich crisis: Sudetenland handed over to Hitler
1939		Hitler over-ran Czechoslovakia
1939–45	SECOND WORLD WAR	
1940–5	*Churchill's first government*	

	Home	*Foreign and Imperial*
	(Coalition)	
1944	Education Act	
1945	*Churchill's second government*	U.N. created
	(Conservative)	
	Sweeping Labour victory in General Election	
1945–51	*Labour government* (Attlee) Policy of nationalisation	
1946	National Insurance Act (coming into operation 1948)	
	National Health Service Act (coming into operation 1948)	
1947		Independence of India and Pakistan
1948		Communists seize power in Czechoslovakia
1948–9		Russians isolated Berlin—Allied air-lift
1949		North Atlantic Treaty signed. N.A.T.O.
		Communist victory in China
1950–3		Korean War (1953 death of Stalin)
1951–5	*Churchill's third government*	
1952	Elizabeth II	
1955–7	*Anthony Eden's government* (Conservative)	
1956		Suez crisis
		Hungarian revolt
1957	*Macmillan's government* (Conservative)	Independence of Ghana
1960		Independence of Nigeria
1961		Russia put man into orbit round earth
1962		U.S. put man into orbit round earth

Some Books Recommended
For Reference or Further Reading

GENERAL

Briggs, Asa. *They Saw It Happen, 1899–1945*. London: Basil Blackwell & Mott, Ltd., 1960.

Ensor, R. C. K. *England, 1870–1914*. New York and London: Oxford University Press, 1936.

Falls, Cyril. *The Great War*. New York: G. P. Putnam's Sons, Inc., 1959; London: Longmans, Green & Co., Ltd., 1960 (as *The First World War*).

See also the rather older histories of the First World War by C. R. M. F. Cruttwell (London: Oxford University Press) and by B. H. Liddell Hart (London: Faber & Faber, Ltd.).

Pelling, Henry. *Modern Britain, 1885–1955*. Edinburgh: Thomas Nelson and Sons, Ltd., 1960; New York: Thomas Nelson and Sons, 1961.

Spender, J. A. *Great Britain: Empire and Commonwealth, 1886–1935*. London: Cassell & Co., Ltd., 1936.

Ashworth, W. *Economic History of England, 1870–1939*. New York: Barnes & Noble, Inc.; London: Methuen & Co., Ltd., 1960.

Bruce, Maurice. *The Coming of the Welfare State*. London: B. T. Batsford, Ltd., 1961.

Derry, T. K. *The United Kingdom—A Survey of British Institutions Today*. London: Longmans, Green & Co., Ltd., 1961; New York: Longmans, Green & Co., Inc., 1962.

Falls, Cyril. *The Second World War*. New York: British Book Centre; London: Methuen & Co., Ltd., 1950.

Mowat, C. L. *Britain Between the Wars, 1918–1940*. Chicago: University of Chicago Press; London: Methuen & Co., Ltd., 1955.

Youngson, A. J. *The British Economy, 1920–1957*. Cambridge, Mass.: Harvard University Press; London: Allen & Unwin, Ltd., 1960.

For recent events reference may be made to *Keesing's Contemporary Archives, The Annual Register, The Statesman's Year-Book* and the annual *Book of the Year* of the *Encyclopaedia Britannica*.

BIOGRAPHIES AND MEMOIRS

Clarke, E. G. *Benjamin Disraeli*. New York: The Macmillan Company; London: John Murray, Ltd., 1954.

Feiling, Keith. *The Life of Neville Chamberlain*. New York: St Martin's Press; London: Macmillan & Co., Ltd., 1946.

Garvin, J. L., and Amery, J. *Joseph Chamberlain*. 4 vols. New York: St Martin's Press; London: Macmillan & Co., Ltd., 1932–51.

Kennedy, A. L. *Salisbury*. Hollywood-by-the-Sea, Fla.: Transatlantic Arts, Inc.; London: John Murray, Ltd., 1953.

Magnus, Philip. *Gladstone*. New York: E. P. Dutton & Co., Inc.; London: John Murray, Ltd., 1954.

Spender, J. A. *The Life of Sir Henry Campbell-Bannerman*. 2 vols. London: Hodder & Stoughton, Ltd., 1923; Boston: Houghton Mifflin Company, 1924.

Spender, J. A., and Asquith, Cyril. *The Life of Herbert Henry Asquith*. 2 vols. London: Hutchinson & Co., Ltd., 1932.

Thomson, Malcolm. *David Lloyd George*. London: Hutchinson & Co., Ltd., 1948.

Among the many memoirs:

Churchill, Winston. *The World Crisis*. 5 vols. New York: Charles Scribner's Sons, 1923–29; London: Butterworth & Co., Ltd., 1923–31.

———. *The Second World War*. 6 vols. Boston: Houghton Mifflin Company, 1948–53.

Eden, A. *Full Circle*. Boston: Houghton Mifflin Company, 1960. Deals with the years after 1951.

For the Labour Party:

Dalton, Hugh. *Call Back Yesterday: Memoirs*. 3 vols. London: Frederick Muller, Ltd., 1953–62.

Snowden, Philip. *Autobiography*. 2 vols. London: Ivor Nicholson & Watson, Ltd., 1937.

FOREIGN POLICY AND THE EUROPEAN BACKGROUND

Carr, E. H. *International Relations Between the Two World Wars (1919–1939)*. New York and London: The Macmillan Company, 1947.

Derry, T. K., and Jarman, T. L. *The European World, 1870–1961*. Rev. ed. London: G. Bell & Sons, Ltd., 1962.

Jarman, T. L. *The Rise and Fall of Nazi Germany*. London: Cresset Press, Ltd., 1955; New York: New York University Press, 1956; The New American Library (Signet Books), 1961.

Seton-Watson, R. W. *Britain in Europe*. New York and London: Cambridge University Press, 1937.

———. *Britain and the Dictators*. New York and London: Cambridge University Press, 1938.

ASPECTS OF THE AGE

Harrod, R. F. *Life of John Maynard Keynes*. New York: Harcourt, Brace & Co., Inc.; London: Macmillan & Co., Ltd., 1951.

Somervell, D. C. *English Thought in the Nineteenth Century*. Rev. ed. New York: Longmans, Green & Co., Inc., 1948; London: Methuen & Co., Ltd., 1954.

———. *British Politics Since 1900*. New York: Oxford University Press; London: Andrew Dakers, Ltd., 1950.

Spender, Stephen. *World Within World*. New York: Harcourt, Brace & Co., Inc.; London: Hamish Hamilton, Ltd., 1951.

Young, G. M. *Victorian England: Portrait of an Age*. 2nd ed. New York and London: Oxford University Press, 1953; New York: Doubleday & Co., Inc. (Anchor Books), 1954.

Index